SpringerBriefs in Computer Science

T0214581

For further volumes:
http://www.springer.com/series/10028

Xuan Guang • Zhen Zhang

Linear Network Error
Correction Coding

Springer

Xuan Guang
Department of Information and Probability
  School of Mathematical Sciences
Nankai University
Tianjin, People's Republic of China

Zhen Zhang
Ming Hsieh Department of Electrical
  Engineering Viterbi School
  of Engineering
University of Southern California
Los Angeles, CA, USA

ISSN 2191-5768   ISSN 2191-5776 (electronic)
ISBN 978-1-4939-0587-4 ISBN 978-1-4939-0588-1 (eBook)
DOI 10.1007/978-1-4939-0588-1
Springer New York Heidelberg Dordrecht London

Library of Congress Control Number: 2014933580

Printed on acid-free paper

Springer is part of Springer Science+Business Media (www.springer.com)

Contents

Chapter 1
Introduction

In the past two decades, there has been a surge in research activities on coding in communication networks due to its importance in applications. This recent network coding theory reveals a surprising fact that unlike what was believed in the past, optimal information transmission over networks can not always be achieved by routing and replication of the data (or store-and-forward), rather it needs coding. To be specific, in the routing method, data received from an input channel of an internal node are stored and a copy is forwarded to the next node via an output channel. When one internal node has more than one output channel, it sends the copies of the data onto output channels. It has been a folklore in data communications. The network coding theory indicates that it does not suffice to simply route information within a network and its advantage over routing refutes this aforementioned folklore. From then on, network coding has been studied widely and become a new paradigm that has influenced information and coding theory, networking, switching, communications, cryptography, data storage, multimedia and so on.

Network coding allows the internal nodes of a network to process the information received. This idea can be dated back to the works by Yeung and Zhang in [53, 56, 57]. Based on these works, Ahlswede et al. [1] studied the information flow in an arbitrary acyclic network with a single source whose data is multicast to a collection of destinations called sinks or sink nodes. They showed that if coding is applied at nodes in a network, rather than routing alone, the source node can multicast information to all sink nodes at the theoretically maximum information rate as the alphabet size approaches infinity, where the theoretically maximum rate is the smallest minimum cut capacity between the source node and any sink node.

Further, a well-known example of the butterfly network, depicted in Fig. 1.1, was proposed to characterize the advantage of network coding which later became the classical "trademark" for network coding. This is one of the simplest and the most classical examples, which shows that data processing or coding at internal nodes can help increase the data transmission throughput. In the network, there is a single source s, which generates bits a and b, and two sinks t_1 and t_2 both of which request both bits a and b. And each edge in the network has capacity to transmit one single bit at a time. First, we try to derive a routing (store-and-forward) scheme for this

X. Guang and Z. Zhang, *Linear Network Error Correction Coding*, SpringerBriefs in Computer Science, DOI 10.1007/978-1-4939-0588-1_1, © The Author(s) 2014

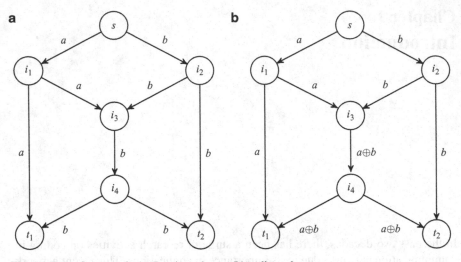

Fig. 1.1 Butterfly network. (**a**) Routing scheme, (**b**) coding scheme

purpose as shown by Fig. 1.1a. By symmetric, the source s sends the two bits on outgoing channels, without loss of generality, a is sent on channel (s, i_1), b is sent on channel (s, i_2). At internal nodes i_1 and i_2, the received bit is replicated and the copies are sent on the two outgoing channels. At internal node i_3, since both a and b are received but there is only one outgoing channel, we have to choose one of the two bits to be sent on the channel (i_3, i_4). Thus, there is a bottleneck here. Suppose that b is sent on (i_3, i_4). The node i_4 receives and replicates the bit b, and the two copies are further sent to t_1 and t_2, respectively. At sink node t_1, both a and b are received. However, the sink node t_2 only receives two copies of the bit b. Thus, the routing scheme does not work. Similarly, if a instead of b is sent on (i_3, i_4), then t_1 can not obtain the bit b. On the other hand, if coding is allowed, it is actually possible to achieve our goal as shown by Fig. 1.1b. Specifically, the node i_3 can simply transmit the sum $a \oplus b$ of the bits a and b, where $\oplus$ denotes modulo 2 addition. This allows t_1 to recover b, because

$$a \oplus (a \oplus b) = (a \oplus a) \oplus b = b,$$

and, similarly, t_2 to recover $a = (a \oplus b) \oplus b$. Thus, network coding overcomes this bottleneck and actually increase the throughput of a communication network.

1.1 Linear Network Coding

First, we give some notation frequently used in this book. A communication network is defined as a finite acyclic directed graph $G = (V, E)$, where the vertex set V stands for the set of nodes and the edge set E represents the set of communication channels of the network. In this book, we only consider acyclic networks, i.e., networks with no directed cycle. The node set V consists of three disjoint subsets S, T, and J, where S is the set of source nodes, T is the set of sink nodes, and $J = V - S - T$ is the set of internal nodes. The source nodes generate messages and transmit them to all sink nodes over the network. In addition, we only consider single source networks, i.e., $|S| = 1$, and the unique source node is denoted by s. A direct edge $e = (i,j) \in E$ represents a channel leading from node i to node j. Node i is called the tail of e and node j is called the head of e, written as $i = tail(e)$, $j = head(e)$, respectively. Correspondingly, the channel e is called an outgoing channel of i and an incoming channel of j. For a node i, define

$$Out(i) = \{e \in E : e \text{ is an outgoing channel of } i\} = \{e \in E : tail(e) = i\},$$
$$In(i) = \{e \in E : e \text{ is an incoming channel of } i\} = \{e \in E : head(e) = i\}.$$

Note that the source node s has no incoming channels and any sink node has no outgoing channels. In a communication network, if a sequence of channels $(e_1, e_2, \cdots, e_m)$ satisfies $tail(e_1) = i$, $head(e_m) = j$, and $tail(e_{k+1}) = head(e_k)$ for $k = 1, 2, \cdots, m - 1$, then we call the sequence $(e_1, e_2, \cdots, e_m)$ a path from node i to node j, or a path from channel e_1 to node j. For each channel $e \in E$, there exists a positive number R_e called the capacity of e. We allow the multiple channels between two nodes and assume reasonably that the capacity of any channel is 1 per unit time. This means that one field symbol can be transmitted over a channel in one unit time.

A cut between node i and node j is a set of channels whose removal disconnects i from j. For unit capacity channels, the capacity of a cut can be regarded as the number of channels in the cut, and the minimum of all capacities of cuts between i and j is called the minimum cut capacity between node i and node j. A cut between node i and node j is called a minimum cut if its capacity achieves the minimum cut capacity between i and j. Note that there may exist several minimum cuts between i and j, but the minimum cut capacity between them is determined.

In a linear network code, information symbols are regarded as elements of a finite field $\mathscr{F}$, which is called base field of this linear network code. These information symbols includes the symbols generated by the source node and the symbols transmitted on the channels. Furthermore, encoding and decoding are based on the linear algebra defined on the base field. In addition, we make an ideal and reasonable assumption that the propagation delay in the network, which includes the coding operations delay at the nodes and the transmission delay over the channels, is zero, since acyclic networks are under consideration. Following the direction of the channels, there is an upstream-to-downstream order (ancestral topological order) on the channels in E which is consistent with the partial order of all channels. The coordinates of all vectors and rows/columns of all matrices in this book are indexed according to this upstream-to-downstream order, unless otherwise mentioned. In particular, if L is such a matrix whose column vectors are indexed by a collection $B \subseteq E$ of channels according to an upstream-to-downstream order, then we use some symbol with subscript e, $e \in B$, such as l_e, to denote the column vector corresponding to the channel e, and the matrix L is written as a column-vector form $L = \begin{bmatrix} l_e : & e \in B \end{bmatrix}$.

And if L is a matrix whose row vectors are indexed by this collection B of channels, then we use some symbol with e inside a pair of brackets, such as $l(e)$, to denote the row vector corresponding to e, and the matrix L is written as a row-vector form $L = \left[l(e) : e \in B \right]$. Further, throughout this book, we use $\mathbf{0}$ to represent an all zero row/column vector, or an all zero matrix sometimes, whose size is always clear from the context.

Next, we formulate a linear network code over an acyclic network G. Encoding at the nodes (including the source node) in the network is carried out according to a certain upstream-to-downstream order. At a node in the network, the ensemble of received symbols are linearly mapped to a symbol in $\mathscr{F}$ specific to each output channel, and the symbol is sent on that channel. To be specific, the source node generates the original messages and we use the concept of imaginary incoming channels of the source node s. Assume that these imaginary incoming channels provide the source messages to s. Let the information rate be ω symbols per unit time. Then the source node has ω imaginary incoming channels $d'_1, d'_2, \cdots, d'_\omega$ and let $In(s) = \{d'_1, d'_2, \cdots, d'_\omega\}$. The source messages are ω symbols $\mathbf{x} = (x_1\, x_2\, \cdots\, x_\omega)$ arranged in a row vector where each x_i is an element of the base field $\mathscr{F}$. Subsequently, they are assumed to transmit to the source node s through the ω imaginary channels in $In(s)$, and without loss of generality, the message transmitted over the ith imaginary channel is the ith source message. Further, at each node $i \in V - T$ (including the source node s), there is an $|In(i)| \times |Out(i)|$ matrix $K_i = (k_{d,e})_{d \in In(i), e \in Out(i)}$, say the local encoding kernel at i, where $k_{d,e} \in \mathscr{F}$ is called the local encoding coefficient for the adjacent pair (d,e) of channels d, e. Denote by U_e the message transmitted over the channel e. Hence, at the source node, we have $U_{d'_i} = x_i$, $1 \leq i \leq \omega$. In general, the message U_e is calculated recursively by the formula

$$U_e = \sum_{d \in In(tail(e))} k_{d,e} U_d.$$

Furthermore, it is not difficult to see that U_e, actually, is a linear combination of the ω source symbols x_i, $1 \leq i \leq \omega$. Hence, there is an ω-dimensional column vector f_e over the base field $\mathscr{F}$ such that $U_e = \mathbf{x} \cdot f_e$ (see also [52, 55]). This column vector f_e is called the global encoding kernel of the channel e and it can be determined by the local encoding kernels. The following example illustrates a linear network code over the butterfly network as described in Fig. 1.1.

Example 1.1. Let $\mathbf{x} = (x_1\, x_2) \in \mathbb{F}_2^2$ be two-dimensional message vector generated by the source node s. Figure 1.2 shows a two-dimensional binary linear network code over the butterfly network. The local encoding kernels at the nodes are respective:

$$K_s = \begin{bmatrix} 1 & 0 \\ 0 & 1 \end{bmatrix}, \; K_{i_1} = K_{i_2} = K_{i_4} = \begin{bmatrix} 1 & 1 \end{bmatrix}, \; K_{i_3} = \begin{bmatrix} 1 \\ 1 \end{bmatrix}.$$

The global encoding kernels for all channels are respective:

$$f_{e_1} = f_{e_3} = f_{e_4} = \begin{bmatrix} 1 \\ 0 \end{bmatrix}, \; f_{e_2} = f_{e_5} = f_{e_6} = \begin{bmatrix} 0 \\ 1 \end{bmatrix}, \; f_{e_7} = f_{e_8} = f_{e_9} = \begin{bmatrix} 1 \\ 1 \end{bmatrix}.$$

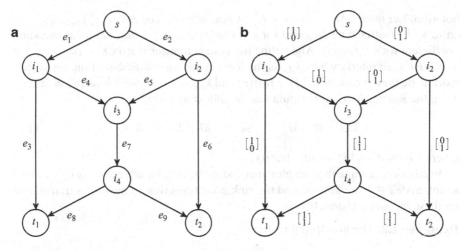

Fig. 1.2 A linear network code over the butterfly network. (**a**) Butterfly network G, (**b**) the global encoding kernels

In the following, the definition of a linear network code is presented formally by both local and global descriptions.

Definition 1.1.

Local Description of a Linear Network Code. An ω-dimensional linear network code on an acyclic network over a base field $\mathscr{F}$ consists of a scalar encoding coefficient $k_{d,e} \in \mathscr{F}$ for every adjacent pair (d,e) of channels in the network. The $|In(i)| \times |Out(i)|$ matrix

$$K_i = (k_{d,e})_{d\in In(i), e\in Out(i)}$$

is called the local encoding kernel at the node i. All local encoding kernels constitute a local description of a linear network code.

Global Description of a Linear Network Code. An ω-dimensional linear network code on an acyclic network over a base field $\mathscr{F}$ consists of a scalar $k_{d,e} \in \mathscr{F}$ for every adjacent pair (d,e) of channels in the network as well as an ω-dimensional column vector f_e for each channel e such that:

- $f_e = \sum_{d\in In(tail(e))} k_{d,e} f_d$;
- The vectors $f_{d'_i}$, $1 \le i \le \omega$, for the ω imaginary channels in $In(s)$ form the standard basis of the vector space $\mathscr{F}^\omega$.

The vector f_e is called the global encoding kernel of the channel e. All global encoding kernels constitute a global description of a linear network code.

Furthermore, there is an equality below characterizing the relation between local encoding kernels and global encoding kernels, which was proposed by Koetter and Médard [31]. Thus, we say it Koetter-Médard Formula. First, we introduce some notation. Let matrix $M = \begin{bmatrix} f_e : e \in E \end{bmatrix}$ of size $\omega \times |E|$, and $B = (k_{d,e})_{d \in In(s), e \in E}$ be an $\omega \times |E|$ matrix with $k_{d,e} = 0$ for $e \notin Out(s)$ and $k_{d,e}$ being the local encoding coefficient for $e \in Out(s)$. And define the system transfer matrix $K = (k_{d,e})_{d \in E, e \in E}$ as an $|E| \times |E|$ matrix where $k_{d,e}$ is the local encoding coefficient of the linear network code for the case $head(d) = tail(e)$ and $k_{d,e} = 0$ otherwise $head(d) \neq tail(e)$. Then the Koetter-Médard Formula has the following form:

$$MK + B = M, \qquad \text{or} \qquad M = B \cdot (I - K)^{-1}, \qquad (1.1)$$

where I is an $|E| \times |E|$ identity matrix.

In addition, assume that the global encoding kernels for all incoming channels of a sink node $t \in T$ are known, and the sink node t receives all messages transmitted on these incoming channels.

Definition 1.2. The $\omega \times |In(t)|$ matrix

$$F_t = \begin{bmatrix} f_e : e \in In(t) \end{bmatrix}$$

is called the decoding matrix at the sink node $t \in T$. Let an $|In(t)|$-dimensional received vector be

$$\mathbf{y}_t = \begin{bmatrix} U_e : e \in In(t) \end{bmatrix}.$$

The equation

$$\mathbf{y}_t = \mathbf{x} \cdot F_t$$

is called the decoding equation at the sink node $t \in T$.

This implies that the sink node t can decode the original source message vector $\mathbf{x}$ successfully if and only if $\text{Rank}(F_t) = \omega$. By [1, 33], we can obtain the following famous linear network coding theorem.

Theorem 1.1 (Linear Network Coding Theorem). *Let $G = (V, E)$ be a single source multicast acyclic network with unit channel capacity for each channel $e \in E$ and $\mathscr{F}$ be the base field satisfying its size more than the number of the sink nodes. Then the information rate ω is achievable, i.e., there exists a linear network code over the field $\mathscr{F}$ such that each sink node $t \in T$ can decode the ω-dimensional original message vectors successfully, if and only if*

$$\omega \leq \min_{t \in T} \text{mincut}(s, t),$$

where $\text{mincut}(s, t)$ represents the minimum cut capacity between s and t.

Before proving this theorem, the following lemma is required.

Lemma 1.1. *Let $f(x_1, x_2, \cdots, x_n) \in \mathscr{F}[x_1, x_2, \cdots, x_n]$ be a nonzero polynomial with coefficients in the field $\mathscr{F}$. If the highest degree of f in every x_i for $1 \leq i \leq n$ is less than the size of the field, then there exist $a_1, a_2, \cdots, a_n \in \mathscr{F}$ such that*

$$f(a_1, a_2, \cdots, a_n) \neq 0.$$

Proof. We will prove this lemma by induction. First, for $n = 1$, the lemma is evident as the fact that the number of roots of a nonzero polynomial $f(x) \in \mathscr{F}[x]$ is no more than its degree. Further, assume that the lemma is true for $n - 1$ for some $n > 1$. Express $f(x_1, x_2, \cdots, x_n)$ as polynomial on x_n with coefficients in the polynomial ring $\mathscr{F}[x_1, x_2, \cdots, x_{n-1}]$, i.e.,

$$f(x_1, x_2, \cdots, x_n)$$
$$= h_k(x_1, x_2, \cdots, x_{n-1})x_n^k + h_{k-1}(x_1, x_2, \cdots, x_{n-1})x_n^{k-1} + \cdots + h_0(x_1, x_2, \cdots, x_{n-1}),$$

where k is the degree of f in x_n and the leading coefficient $h_k(x_1, x_2, \cdots, x_{n-1})$ is a nonzero polynomial in $\mathscr{F}[x_1, x_2, \cdots, x_{n-1}]$. By the induction hypothesis, there exist $a_1, a_2, \cdots, a_{n-1} \in \mathscr{F}$ such that $h_k(a_1, a_2, \cdots, a_{n-1}) \neq 0$ as the degree of h_k in each x_i is no more than the degree of f in each x_i, where $1 \leq i \leq n - 1$. Hence,

$$f(a_1, a_2, \cdots, a_{n-1}, x_n)$$
$$= h_k(a_1, a_2, \cdots, a_{n-1})x_n^k + h_{k-1}(a_1, a_2, \cdots, a_{n-1})x_n^{k-1} + \cdots + h_0(a_1, a_2, \cdots, a_{n-1}),$$

is a nonzero polynomial in $\mathscr{F}[x_n]$ with degree k less than $|\mathscr{F}|$, which implies that these exists $a_n \in \mathscr{F}$ such that

$$f(a_1, a_2, \cdots, a_{n-1}, a_n) \neq 0.$$

This completes the proof. $\square$

Now we start to prove the theorem.

Proof (Proof of Theorem 1.1). First, assume that the information rate ω is achievable, that is, there exist a linear network code such that each sink node $t \in T$ can decode successfully for this rate ω, or equivalently, the decoding matrix F_t is full rank for each sink $t \in T$, i.e., $\mathrm{Rank}(F_t) = \omega$, where recall that $F_t = [f_e : e \in In(t)]$.

Further, let $CUT(s,t)$ be an arbitrary cut between the source node s and the sink node $t \in T$. It is not difficult to see that the global encoding kernel f_e for each $e \in In(t)$ is a linear combination of global encoding kernels in $\{f_e : e \in CUT(s,t)\}$. In other words, the vector space $\langle\{f_e : e \in In(t)\}\rangle^1$ is a subspace of the vector space $\langle\{f_e : e \in CUT(s,t)\}\rangle$, which leads to

$$\omega = \mathrm{Rank}(F_t)$$
$$= \dim(\langle\{f_e : e \in In(t)\}\rangle)$$
$$\leq \dim(\langle\{f_e : e \in CUT(s,t)\}\rangle)$$
$$\leq |CUT(s,t)|.$$

Minimizing over all the cuts between s and t, we have

$$\omega \leq \mathrm{mincut}(s,t).$$

---

[1] Let L be a collection of vectors in some linear space. As convenience, we use $\langle L \rangle$ to represent the subspace spanned by the vectors in L.

Furthermore, minimizing over all sink nodes $t \in T$, it follows

$$\omega \leq \min_{t \in T} \text{mincut}(s,t).$$

On the other hand, we assume that $\omega \leq \min_{t \in T} \text{mincut}(s,t)$. Hence, for any sink node $t \in T$, there exist ω channel-disjoint paths from s to t denoted by $P_{t,1}, P_{t,2}, \cdots, P_{t,\omega}$. Further, denote by $e_{t,i}$ the last channel on the ith path $P_{t,i}$ for $1 \leq i \leq \omega$, and note that $e_{t,i} \in In(t)$. Without loss of generality, assume that the order of these channels satisfy $e_{t,1} \prec e_{t,2} \prec \cdots \prec e_{t,\omega}$, and let $In'(t) = \{e_{t,1}, e_{t,2}, \cdots, e_{t,\omega}\}$. Then, clearly, $In'(t) \subseteq In(t)$.

Subsequently, let $F'_t = [f_e : e \in In'(t)]$, and then F'_t has size $\omega \times \omega$ and is a submatrix of F_t. This implies that $\text{Rank}(F_t) = \omega$ provided $\text{Rank}(F'_t) = \omega$. Therefore, it suffices to find $k_{d,e} \in \mathscr{F}$ such that $\text{Rank}(F'_t) = \omega$ for each sink node $t \in T$, or equivalently, find $k_{d,e} \in \mathscr{F}$ such that $\det(F'_t) \neq 0$ for any $t \in T$, i.e., $\prod_{t \in T} \det(F'_t) \neq 0$. Thus, we naturally regard $\prod_{t \in T} \det(F'_t)$ as a polynomial over the field $\mathscr{F}$ with all the $k_{d,e}$ as indeterminates.

First, we indicate that $\prod_{t \in T} \det(F'_t)$ is a nonzero polynomial. For any $t \in T$, recall that $P_{t,1}, P_{t,2}, \cdots, P_{t,\omega}$ are ω channel-disjoint paths from s to t. Assign the imaginary channel d'_i to the path $P_{t,i}$ for $1 \leq i \leq \omega$ in order to obtain ω channel-disjoint paths from $In(s) = \{d'_1, d'_2, \cdots, d'_\omega\}$ to t, and denote them by $P'_{t,i}$, $1 \leq i \leq \omega$. Define

$$k_{d,e} = \begin{cases} 1 & \text{if } (d,e) \text{ is an adjacent pair of channels on some path } P'_{t,i}, \ 1 \leq i \leq \omega, \\ 0 & \text{otherwise.} \end{cases}$$

Thus, it is not difficult to see that in this case $F'_t = I_{\omega \times \omega}$, i.e., $\det(F'_t) = 1$, which means that $\det(F'_t)$ is a nonzero polynomial over $\mathscr{F}$. Notice that it is true for each sink $t \in T$. So it follows that $\prod_{t \in T} \det(F'_t)$ is a nonzero polynomial, too.

Next, it suffices to prove that when $|\mathscr{F}| > |T|$, there exist $k_{d,e} \in \mathscr{F}$ such that $\prod_{t \in T} \det(F'_t) \neq 0$. Recall Koetter-Médard formula (1.1): $M = B(I - K)^{-1}$, and define an $\omega \times |E|$ matrix $A_{In'(t)} = (A_{d,e})_{d \in In'(t), e \in E}$, where

$$A_{d,e} = \begin{cases} 1 & d = e; \\ 0 & \text{otherwise.} \end{cases}$$

Hence,

$$F'_t = MA_{In'(t)}^\top = B(I - K)^{-1} A_{In'(t)}^\top. \tag{1.2}$$

Consider the determinant of an $(\omega + |E|) \times (\omega + |E|)$ matrix below:

$$\det \left(\begin{bmatrix} B & \mathbf{0}_{\omega \times \omega} \\ I - K & A_{In'(t)}^\top \end{bmatrix} \right)$$

$$= \det \left(\begin{bmatrix} B & -B(I-K)^{-1}A_{In'(t)}^\top \\ I - K & \mathbf{0}_{|E| \times \omega} \end{bmatrix} \right)$$

$$= (-1)^* \det((I - K)) \cdot \det(B(I-K)^{-1}A_{In'(t)}^\top)$$

$$= \det(F'_t) \cdot (-1)^*, \tag{1.3}$$

where $\mathbf{0}_{a \times b}$ represents an all zero matrix of size $a \times b$, and the equality (1.3) follows from (1.2) and $\det((I - K)) = 1$ because K is an upper triangular matrix and all elements of main diagonal are zeros. This implies that the degree of each indeterminate $k_{d,e}$ in the polynomial $\det(F_t')$ is one at most, which further induces the degree of each indeterminate $k_{d,e}$ in the polynomial $\prod_{t \in T} \det(F_t')$ no more than $|T|$. Together with Lemma 1.1, this proves that there exist $k_{d,e} \in \mathscr{F}$ such that $\prod_{t \in T} \det(F_t') \neq 0$, provided that $|\mathscr{F}| > |T|$. This completes the proof. $\square$

1.2 Construction of Linear Network Codes

Actually, the proof of the sufficiency in Theorem 1.1 describes the existence of a linear network code by an algebraic method. The Algorithm 1 constructs a linear network code deterministically in polynomial time. Unlike the algebraic approach given in the proof of Theorem 1.1 that assigns values to the local encoding coefficients, this algorithm assigns values to the global encoding kernels, that is usually called Jaggi-Sanders Algorithm.

Algorithm Verification. In the updating process, if (1.4) holds, i.e., we always can choose f_e satisfying (1.4), then $\{f_e, e \in CUT_t\}$ are always linearly independent for each $t \in T$. By Algorithm 1, we know $CUT_t \subseteq In(t)$ at the end. Thus, the matrix $[f_e : e \in CUT_t]$ is a submatrix of F_t, together with $\text{Rank}\left([f_e : e \in CUT_t]\right) = \omega$, which implies that $\text{Rank}(F_t) = \omega$ for any sink node $t \in T$.

Next, the remaining is to prove that (1.4) holds provided $|\mathscr{F}| > |T|$, which is equivalent to prove

$$|\mathscr{L}(In(i)) \setminus \cup_{t:\ t \in T \text{ and } e \in E_t} \mathscr{L}(CUT_t \setminus \{e(t)\})| > 0.$$

Assume $\dim(\mathscr{L}(In(i))) = k$. Note that $f_{e(t)} \in \mathscr{L}(In(i))$ as $e(t) \in In(i)$ for $e \in E_t$, and $f_{e(t)}$ and $\{f_e : e \in CUT_t \setminus \{e(t)\}\}$ are linearly independent since $|CUT_t| = \dim(\mathscr{L}(CUT_t)) = \omega$. This implies that

$$\dim(\mathscr{L}(In(i)) \cap \mathscr{L}(CUT_t \setminus \{e(t)\})) \leq k - 1.$$

Therefore,

$$|\mathscr{L}(In(i)) \setminus \cup_{t:\ t \in T \text{ and } e \in E_t} \mathscr{L}(CUT_t \setminus \{e(t)\})|$$
$$= |\mathscr{L}(In(i))| - |\mathscr{L}(In(i)) \cap (\cup_{t:\ t \in T \text{ and } e \in E_t} \mathscr{L}(CUT_t \setminus \{e(t)\}))|$$
$$= |\mathscr{L}(In(i))| - |\cup_{t:\ t \in T \text{ and } e \in E_t} (\mathscr{L}(In(i)) \cap \mathscr{L}(CUT_t \setminus \{e(t)\}))|$$
$$\geq |\mathscr{F}|^k - \sum_{t \in T} |\mathscr{F}|^{k-1}$$
$$= |\mathscr{F}|^{k-1} (|\mathscr{F}| - |T|) > 0.$$

Algorithm 1 Jaggi-Sanders Algorithm for constructing a linear network code

---
Input:

- A communication network $G = (V, E)$ with the source node s and the set T of sink nodes;
- Base field $\mathscr{F}$ satisfying $|\mathscr{F}| > |T|$;
- The information rate ω with $\omega \leq \min_{t \in T} \text{mincut}(s, t)$.

Output: All global encoding kernels $\{f_e : e \in E\}$ constituting a global description of a linear network code.

Initialization:

1. For each $t \in T$, find ω channel-disjoint paths $P_{t,1}, P_{t,2}, \cdots, P_{t,\omega}$ from $In(s)$ to t, and denote the set of them by $\mathscr{P}_t$. Use E_t to denote the set of all channels on $\mathscr{P}_t$;
2. For each $t \in T$, define a dynamic channel-set CUT_t, and initialize it as $CUT_t = In(s) = \{d'_1, d'_2, \cdots, d'_\omega\}$. Let the global encoding kernels $f_{d'_i} = 1_{d'_i}$ for $1 \leq i \leq \omega$, where $1_{d'_i}$ is an indicator function of imaginary channel d'_i.

1: **for each** node $i \in V$ (according to the given ancestral order of nodes) **do**
2:      **for each** channel $e \in Out(i)$ **do**
3:          **if** $e \notin \cup_{t \in T} E_t$ **then**
4:              $f_e = \mathbf{0}$, and all CUT_t remain unchanged.
5:          **else if** $e \in \cup_{t \in T} E_t$ **then**
6:              choose arbitrarily

$$f_e \in \mathscr{L}(In(i)) \backslash \cup_{t:\ t \in T\ \text{and}\ e \in E_t} \mathscr{L}(CUT_t \backslash \{e(t)\}), \qquad (1.4)$$

            where $\mathscr{L}(D)$ represents a vector space spanned by the global encoding kernels for the channels in a channel set $D \subseteq E$, i.e., $\mathscr{L}(D) = \langle \{f_e : e \in D\} \rangle$, and $e(t)$ denotes the previous channel of e on the path in $\mathscr{P}_t$ on which e locates.
7:          For those CUT_t satisfying $e \in E_t$, update $CUT_t = \{CUT_t \backslash \{e(t)\}\} \cup \{e\}$, and for others, CUT_t remain unchanged.
8:      **end if**
9:      **end for**
10: **end for**

1.3 Random Network Coding

It must be noted that the linear network codes discussed above, either the algebraic approach or the constructive algorithm, are designed based on the global network topology. However, for many communication networks in practice, the network topology cannot be utilized, for instance, the network is huge in scale, or complicated in structure, even dynamic. So it is impossible to use the predesigned codes based on network topology in these cases even if the network topology is known. In order to deal with this problem, Ho et al. [19, 22] proposed random linear network coding as an acceptable coding technique. The main idea is that when a node (maybe the source node s) receives the messages from its all incoming channels, for each outgoing channel, it randomly and uniformly picks the encoding coefficients from the base field $\mathscr{F}$, uses them to encode the received messages, and transmits the encoded messages over the outgoing channel. In other words, the local coding coefficients $k_{d,e}$ are independently and uniformly distributed random variables taking values in the base field $\mathcal{F}$. Since random linear network coding does not consider the global network topology or coordinate codings at different nodes, it may not achieve the best possible performance of network coding, that is, some sink nodes may not decode correctly. Hence, the performance analysis of random linear network coding is important in theory and application. It is characterized by widely studying the different failure probabilities including failure probability at sink node, failure probability for networks, and the average failure probability, in a series of papers [2, 15, 16, 19, 22] etc. One of important conclusions on random linear network coding is that this random method can construct decodable linear network codes with probability close to one for sufficiently large base field $\mathcal{F}$.

In network coding, two kinds of network models have been considered: coherent and noncoherent networks. A network is called coherent if network characteristics, including the network topology and the network code, are known to the source node and the sink nodes, and called noncoherent if they are unknown. Generally speaking, when using the deterministic construction of linear network codes, the network transmission is usually considered to be "coherent". For random linear network coding, the network transmission is usually considered to be "noncoherent". However, coherent/noncoherent is not equivalent to deterministic/random. And it is possible to use noncoherent transmission for deterministic linear network codes and use coherent transmission for random linear network codes.

1.4 Network Error Correction Coding

As what we have seen above, the principle of network coding is elegant and compelling. Network coding achieves its benefits, essentially, by encoding the packets transmitted over the networks. In other words, many packets in the network are statistically dependent. This dependence also takes a problem. What if some channels are not error-free, or equivalently, what if some of packets are corrupted? This dependence will lead to an error propagation problem, which is contrast to the routing, where an error in one packet affects only one source-to-sink path. Even a single corrupt packet has potential to corrupt all packets received by a sink node for network coding. In order to deal with this problem, network error correction coding was proposed recently, which introduced redundancies in the space domain instead of in the time domain as the classical error-correcting coding does. In a network communication with network coding, many types of errors may occur.

- **Random Errors.** Generally speaking, random errors are caused by channel noise, the correction of which in end-to-end communication models has been discussed extensively in classical coding theory. For network communication, we may use an error-correcting code with good error detection capability in a packet as local code. When the number of errors in the packet is small, they can be corrected. When the number of errors is large, the errors can be detected with high probability and the corresponding packet is deleted. Only in the case where the errors are undetectable, the erroneous packet remains in the network and affects other packets when network coding is used.

- **Erasure Errors.** Erasure errors, or called packet losses are usually caused by traffic jam in networks. This kind of errors has also been discussed extensively in network theory.
- **Malicious Attack.** This type of errors might be from the presence of an adversary, which does not comply with the protocol. The adversary injects corrupt packets into the channels and his effects cannot possibly be detected. This kind of adversarial errors represents an more severe problem than any other type of errors, since they can be designed specifically to defeat the end-to-end error-correcting codes.
- **Errors in Header.** In a packet, some crucial information, such as the global kernel of the packet in network coding, the place where the packet originated (source node), and the destinations of the packet (sink nodes), are recorded. Any error in the header may cause serious problems for transmission. If the global kernel is altered, it is called a global kernel error, which will affect the decoding at the destination. If the destination information is altered, it may cause packet loss at sink nodes.

As far as we know, the classical error-correcting coding as a powerful tool has been used widely to protect data for the end-to-end channel with noise. But the classical error-correcting coding is no more well-suited to network communication induced by network coding. Traditionally, corrupt packets are dealt with by automatic retransmission query (ARQ) technique, that is, once corrupt packets are detected, they are rejected immediately by the network layer and request for retransmission. First, the physical-layer code may not always be perfect, and very reliable physical-layer codes require very long block length. Further, since detection and retransmission are needed, the long delays may not be avoided. There are many situations where a short block length or a short delay, particularly in delay sensitive applications, are required. Moreover, network error correction code is a suitable candidate to solve the problems of malicious attack, and the problems are unlikely solvable by classical error-correcting codes alone. And the product of classical error-correcting code in the time domain and the network error correction code in the space domain may provide superior performance for correcting errors, that is not achievable by classical error-correcting codes alone.

1.5 Historical Notes

Network coding allows the internal nodes of a network to process the information received. This idea can be dated back to the works by Yeung and Zhang in [53, 56, 57]. Based on these works, Ahlswede et al. [1] fully developed this idea and first used the term "network coding". They studied the information flow in an arbitrary acyclic network with a single source whose data is multicast to sink nodes. Further, a well-known example of the butterfly network, depicted in Fig. 1.1, was proposed to characterize the advantage of network coding which later became the classical "trademark" for network coding. This is one of the simplest and the most classical examples, which shows that data processing or coding at internal nodes can help increase the data transmission throughput.

Following the line of research, Li et al. [33] further indicated that linear network coding with finite alphabet size is sufficient for multicast in single source networks by using a vector space approach. Subsequently, Koetter and Médard [31] presented an algebraic characterization for network coding by using a matrix approach. These two approaches correspond respectively to the notation of global encoding kernels and local encoding kernels. Neither the construction in [33] for a generic network code nor the construction in [31] for a linear multicast is a polynomial-time algorithm. Although network coding can achieve the higher information rates than classical routing, Jaggi et al. [25] still proposed a polynomial-time constructive algorithm for linear network codes. It must be noted that this algorithm is based on the global network topology. For a detail and comprehensive discussion of network coding, refer to books [10, 20, 52, 55].

However, for many network communication problems, the network topology may not be utilized completely. For instance, the network is huge in scale, or complicated in structure, or dynamic. So, in this case, it is impossible to use this pre-designed network code even if the network topology is known. In order to solve this problem, Ho et al. [19, 22] introduced random linear network coding as a feasible coding technique, proved the optimality of random linear network coding, and proposed the use of such codes on networks with unknown topology. The main results of [19, 22] are upper bounds on failure probabilities of the codes and the conclusion that this random method can construct decodable linear network codes with probability close to one for sufficiently large base field $\mathscr{F}$. Further, Balli et al. [2] improved on these bounds for both cases with and without redundancy, and obtained some results on random linear network error correction codes. But the upper bounds on the failure probabilities in either [19] or [2] are not tight. Particularly, the results in [19] apply the number of the channels on networks, and the conclusions in [2] utilize the number of the nodes on network. Following the research line [2], by utilizing channel-disjoint source-to-sink paths, Guang and Fu [15, 16] further gave some tight or asymptotically tight bounds for different kinds of failure probabilities and also indicated the specific network structures of the worst performance.

As mentioned above, all kinds of errors may occur in practical network communication such as random errors, erasure errors (packet losses), errors in headers and so on. In order to deal with such problems, network error correction (NEC) coding was studied recently. The original idea of network error correction coding was proposed by Yeung and Cai in their conference paper [4] and developed in their journal papers [5, 54]. In the latter two papers, the concept of network error correction codes was introduced as a generalization of the classical error-correcting codes [34, 35]. They also extended some important bounds from classical error-correcting codes to network error correction codes, such as the Singleton bound, the Hamming bound, and the Gilbert-Varshamov bound. Although the Singleton bound has been given in Cai and Yeung [54], Zhang [59] and Yang et al. [49, 50] presented the refined Singleton bound independently by using the different methods. Based on the Singleton bound, [18, 38, 50, 59] etc. also studied the existence and the construction of linear network error correction maximum distance separable (MDS) codes which meet the singleton bound with equality. Yang et al. [49, 51] developed a framework for characterizing error correction/detection capabilities of network error correction codes. They defined different minimum distances to measure error correction and error detection capabilities, respectively. It followed an interesting discovery that, for nonlinear network error correction codes, the number of the correctable errors can be more than half of the number of the detectable errors. In [59], Zhang defined the minimum distance of linear network error correction codes and introduced the concept of extended global encoding kernels. Using this concept, Zhang proposed linear network error correction codes in packet networks. Besides coherent networks, this scheme is also suitable to noncoherent networks by recording the extended global encoding kernels in the headers of the packets. Moreover, the extended global encoding kernels are used to form the decoding matrices at sink nodes. As well as in [48], the decoding principles and decoding beyond the error correction capability were studied. The authors further presented several decoding algorithms and analyzed their performance. In addition, Balli et al. [2] and Guang et al. [18] studied the error correction capability of random linear network error correction codes. They gave the probability mass function of the minimum distance of random linear network error correction codes. For the existence of a network error correction code with degradation, the upper bound on the required field size was proposed. In [3], Cai also considered random linear network coding for error correction. For an overview of the development and some contributions in this research direction, refer to the survey paper [61].

In [29, 30], Koetter and Kschischang formulated a different framework for network error correction coding when a noncoherent network model was under consideration where neither source node nor sink node was assumed to have knowledge of the channel transfer characteristic. In other words, the error control problem in random linear network coding was considered. Motivated by the property that linear network coding is vector-space preserving, in their approach the source message is represented by a subspace of a fixed vector space and a basis of the subspace is injected into the network. Thus, this type of network error correction codes is called subspace codes. A metric was proposed to account for the discrepancy between the transmitted and received spaces and a coding theory based on this metric was developed. Sphere-packing and sphere-covering bounds as well as a generalization of the Singleton bound were given for subspace codes. In particularly, a nearly optimal Reed-Solomon-like code is proposed. Silva et al. [41–43] (see also [27, 40]) developed this approach further and explored the close relationship between subspace codes and codes for the rank metric.

Another important class of errors are corrupted packets from malicious nodes. Recent papers [14, 21, 24, 26, 28, 39, 44] discussed this topic from various aspects of the problem and proposed solution methods. The malicious nodes may inject harmful packets to the information flow, which may contaminate other packets because of network coding. This is known as Byzantine attacks. The malicious node may also alter the packets received to intervene the data transmission. Anyway, the goal of them is to interrupt the data transmission. How to deal with this kind of attacks from malicious nodes is one important issue for network coding. Network error correction coding is one possible approach for dealing with this problem by treating the harmful packets injected or altered by the attacker as packets containing errors. Other approaches include, for instance, the detection of the malicious nodes or the packets from the malicious nodes. Some detect the presence of an adversary [21] by incorporating a simple polynomial hash/check value in each packet so that Byzantine modifications can be detected with high probability. This can also be done by some other classical cryptographic techniques [6, 63]. Some tried to locate the malicious attackers so that they could be isolated from the network in the future [39]. Others correct the errors that the malicious node injects into the information flow under specific conditions [14, 23, 24] or to limit their impact [26].

Chapter 2
Network Error Correction Model

In the last chapter, we introduced network coding, and particularly, described linear network coding. From this chapter, we begin to discuss network error correction coding specifically. To be similar, let a communication network be represented by a finite acyclic directed graph with unit capacity channels. The network is used for single source multicast: there is a single source node, which produces messages, and multiple sink nodes, all of which demand the messages. All the remaining nodes are internal nodes. In this chapter, we will give the basic model of network error correction.

2.1 Basic Model

For the case that there is an error on a channel e, the channel model is additive, i.e., the output of the channel e is $\tilde{U}_e = U_e + z_e$, where $U_e \in \mathscr{F}$ is the message that should be transmitted on e and $z_e \in \mathscr{F}$ is the error occurred on e. Further, let error vector be an $|E|$-dimensional row vector $\mathbf{z} = [z_e : e \in E]$ over the field $\mathscr{F}$ with each component z_e representing the error occurred on the corresponding channel e.

Recall some notation in linear network coding, which will be used frequently during our discussion on network error correction coding. The system transfer matrix (also called one-step transfer matrix) $K = (k_{d,e})_{d \in E, e \in E}$ is an $|E| \times |E|$ matrix with $k_{d,e}$ being the local encoding coefficient for $head(d) = tail(e)$ and $k_{d,e} = 0$ for $head(d) \neq tail(e)$. As the transfer from all channels are accumulated, the overall transform matrix is $F = I + K + K^2 + K^3 + \cdots$. And further because the network is finite and acyclic, $K^N = 0$ for some positive integer N. Thus we can write

$$F = I + K + K^2 + K^3 + \cdots = (I - K)^{-1}.$$

X. Guang and Z. Zhang, *Linear Network Error Correction Coding*, SpringerBriefs in Computer Science, DOI 10.1007/978-1-4939-0588-1_2, © The Author(s) 2014

In addition, recall the $\omega \times |E|$ matrix $B = (k_{d,e})_{d \in In(s), e \in E}$ where $k_{d,e} = 0$ for $e \notin Out(s)$ and $k_{d,e}$ is the local encoding coefficient for $e \in Out(s)$. Let $\rho \subseteq E$ represent a set of channels, and for ρ, define a $|\rho| \times |E|$ matrix $A_\rho = (A_{d,e})_{d \in \rho, e \in E}$ satisfying:

$$A_{d,e} = \begin{cases} 1 & d = e; \\ 0 & \text{otherwise.} \end{cases} \tag{2.1}$$

This matrix for different ρ will be used frequently throughout the whole book. Moreover, we say that ρ is an *error pattern* if errors may occur on those channels in it.

Therefore, when a source message vector $\mathbf{x} \in \mathscr{F}^\omega$ is transmitted and an error vector $\mathbf{z} \in \mathscr{F}^{|E|}$ occurs, the received vector $\mathbf{y} \in \mathscr{F}^{|In(t)|}$ at the sink node t is

$$\mathbf{y} = \mathbf{x} \cdot B \cdot F \cdot A_{In(t)}^\top + \mathbf{z} \cdot F \cdot A_{In(t)}^\top. \tag{2.2}$$

Note that the decoding matrix $F_t = [f_e : e \in In(t)] = BFA_{In(t)}^\top$ and further let $G_t \triangleq FA_{In(t)}^\top$. Then the above Eq. (2.2) can be rewritten as

$$\mathbf{y} = \mathbf{x} \cdot F_t + \mathbf{z} \cdot G_t = (\mathbf{x}\ \mathbf{z}) \begin{bmatrix} F_t \\ G_t \end{bmatrix} \triangleq (\mathbf{x}\ \mathbf{z})\tilde{F}_t.$$

Further, let $\mathscr{X}$ be the source message set and $\mathscr{Z}$ be the error vector set. Clearly,

$$\mathscr{X} = \mathscr{F}^\omega \text{ and } \mathscr{Z} = \mathscr{F}^{|E|}.$$

For any sink node $t \in T$, let $\mathscr{Y}_t$ be the received message set with respect to t, that is,

$$\mathscr{Y}_t = \left\{ (\mathbf{x}\ \mathbf{z})\tilde{F}_t : \text{ all } \mathbf{x} \in \mathscr{X}, \mathbf{z} \in \mathscr{Z} \right\}.$$

Furthermore, note that $A_{In(t)}G_t = I_{|In(t)|}$, an $|In(t)| \times |In(t)|$ identity matrix. Hence, for any $\mathbf{y} \in \mathscr{F}^{|In(t)|}$, we at least can choose an error vector $\mathbf{z} \in \mathscr{Z}$ satisfying $\mathbf{z}_{In(t)} = \mathbf{y}$ and $z_e = 0$ for all $e \in E \setminus In(t)$, where $\mathbf{z}_{In(t)}$ only consists of the components corresponding to the channels in $In(t)$, i.e., $\mathbf{z}_{In(t)} = [z_e : e \in In(t)]$, such that

$$\left(\mathbf{0}\ \mathbf{z} \right) \cdot \tilde{F}_t = \mathbf{0}F_t + \mathbf{z}G_t = \mathbf{z}G_t = \mathbf{z}_{In(t)} \cdot A_{In(t)} \cdot G_t = \mathbf{z}_{In(t)} = \mathbf{y}.$$

This shows

$$\begin{aligned} \mathscr{Y}_t &= \left\{ (\mathbf{x}\ \mathbf{z})\tilde{F}_t : \text{ all } \mathbf{x} \in \mathscr{X}, \mathbf{z} \in \mathscr{Z} \right\} \\ &= \{ \mathbf{x}F_t + \mathbf{z}G_t : \text{ all } \mathbf{x} \in \mathscr{X}, \mathbf{z} \in \mathscr{Z} \} \\ &= \mathscr{F}^{|In(t)|}. \end{aligned}$$

Consequently, for each sink node $t \in T$, we define an encoding function $\text{En}^{(t)}$ as follows:

$$\text{En}^{(t)} : \mathscr{X} = \mathscr{F}^\omega \mapsto \mathscr{Y}_t = \mathscr{F}^{|In(t)|}$$

$$\mathbf{x} \mapsto \mathbf{x} \cdot F_t.$$

Definition 2.1. A linear network code is called a regular code, if for any sink node $t \in T$, $\text{Rank}(F_t) = \omega$.

If the considered linear network code is regular, i.e., $\text{Rank}(F_t) = \omega$, $\text{En}^{(t)}$ is an injection, and hence $\text{En}^{(t)}$ is well-defined. Otherwise, if the linear network code is not regular, i.e., $\text{Rank}(F_t) < \omega$ for at least one sink node $t \in T$, then even in the error-free case, the code is not decodable at least one sink node $t \in T$, let alone network error correction. Therefore, we assume that codes considered below are regular. Now, we can define a linear network error correction (LNEC) code as

$$\text{En}^{(t)}(\mathcal{X}) \triangleq \{\text{En}^{(t)}(\mathbf{x}) : \mathbf{x} \in \mathcal{X}\}.$$

To be specific, for any message vector $\mathbf{x} \in \mathcal{F}^\omega$, $\mathbf{x}F_t$ is called a *codeword* for the sink node t, and let

$$\mathscr{C}_t \triangleq \{\mathbf{x}F_t : \text{all } \mathbf{x} \in \mathcal{F}^\omega\},$$

which is the set of all codewords for the sink node $t \in T$, say *codebook* for t.

2.2 Distance and Weight

Similar to the classical coding theory, we can also define the distance between two received vectors at each sink node $t \in T$ in order to characterize their discrepancy.

Definition 2.2. For any two received vectors $\mathbf{y}_1, \mathbf{y}_2 \in \mathcal{F}^{|In(t)|}$ at the sink node $t \in T$, the *distance* between $\mathbf{y}_1$ and $\mathbf{y}_2$ with respect to t is defined as:

$$d^{(t)}(\mathbf{y}_1, \mathbf{y}_2) \triangleq \min\{w_H(\mathbf{z}) : \mathbf{z} \in \mathcal{F}^{|E|} \text{ such that } \mathbf{y}_1 = \mathbf{y}_2 + \mathbf{z}G_t\},$$

where $w_H(\mathbf{z})$ represents the Hamming weight of the error vector $\mathbf{z}$, i.e., the number of nonzero components of $\mathbf{z}$.

In particular, for any two codewords $\mathbf{x}_1F_t$, $\mathbf{x}_2F_t \in \mathscr{C}_t$ (or equivalently, any two message vectors $\mathbf{x}_1, \mathbf{x}_2 \in \mathcal{X}$), the distance between $\mathbf{x}_1F_t$ and $\mathbf{x}_2F_t$ at the sink node $t \in T$ is:

$$d^{(t)}(\mathbf{x}_1F_t, \mathbf{x}_2F_t) = \min\{w_H(\mathbf{z}) : \mathbf{z} \in \mathcal{F}^{|E|} \text{ such that } \mathbf{x}_1F_t = \mathbf{x}_2F_t + \mathbf{z}G_t\}$$
$$= \min\{w_H(\mathbf{z}) : \mathbf{z} \in \mathcal{F}^{|E|} \text{ such that } (\mathbf{x}_1 - \mathbf{x}_2)F_t = \mathbf{z}G_t\}.$$

First, we show that this distance has the following property.

Proposition 2.1. *For any two received vectors* $\mathbf{y}_1, \mathbf{y}_2 \in \mathcal{F}^{|In(t)|}$ *at the sink node* $t \in T$,

$$0 \leq d^{(t)}(\mathbf{y}_1, \mathbf{y}_2) \leq |In(t)|.$$

Proof. We know

$$d^{(t)}(\mathbf{y}_1, \mathbf{y}_2) = \min\{w_H(\mathbf{z}) : \mathbf{z} \in \mathscr{F}^{|E|} \text{ such that } \mathbf{y}_1 = \mathbf{y}_2 + \mathbf{z}G_t\}$$
$$= \min\{w_H(\mathbf{z}) : \mathbf{z} \in \mathscr{F}^{|E|} \text{ such that } \mathbf{y}_1 - \mathbf{y}_2 = \mathbf{z}G_t\},$$

and recall that $A_{In(t)}G_t = I_{|In(t)|}$ is an $|In(t)| \times |In(t)|$ identity matrix. Furthermore, let $\mathbf{z} \in \mathscr{F}^{|E|}$ be an error vector satisfying $\mathbf{z}_{In(t)} = \mathbf{y}_1 - \mathbf{y}_2$ and $z_e = 0$ for all $e \in E \setminus In(t)$. It follows that

$$\mathbf{z} \cdot G_t = \mathbf{z}_{In(t)} \cdot A_{In(t)}G_t = \mathbf{z}_{In(t)} = \mathbf{y}_1 - \mathbf{y}_2,$$

which implies

$$d^{(t)}(\mathbf{y}_1, \mathbf{y}_2) \leq w_H(\mathbf{z}) = w_H(\mathbf{y}_1 - \mathbf{y}_2) \leq |In(t)|.$$

On the other hand, it is evident that $d^{(t)}(\mathbf{y}_1, \mathbf{y}_2) \geq 0$ from $w_H(\mathbf{z}) \geq 0$ for any $\mathbf{z} \in \mathscr{F}^{|E|}$. Combining the above, the proof is completed. $\square$

Further, the following result shows that this distance is an actual metric.

Theorem 2.1. *This distance $d^{(t)}(\cdot, \cdot)$ defined in vector space $\mathscr{F}^{|In(t)|}$ is a metric, that is, the following three properties are qualified. For any $\mathbf{y}_1, \mathbf{y}_2, \mathbf{y}_3$ in $\mathscr{F}^{|In(t)|}$,*

1. **(Positive definiteness)** $d^{(t)}(\mathbf{y}_1, \mathbf{y}_2) \geq 0$, and $d^{(t)}(\mathbf{y}_1, \mathbf{y}_2) = 0$ *if and only if* $\mathbf{y}_1 = \mathbf{y}_2$.
2. **(Symmetry)** $d^{(t)}(\mathbf{y}_1, \mathbf{y}_2) = d^{(t)}(\mathbf{y}_2, \mathbf{y}_1)$.
3. **(Triangle inequality)** $d^{(t)}(\mathbf{y}_1, \mathbf{y}_3) \leq d^{(t)}(\mathbf{y}_1, \mathbf{y}_2) + d^{(t)}(\mathbf{y}_2, \mathbf{y}_3)$.

Thus, the pair $(\mathscr{F}^{|In(t)|}, d^{(t)})$ is a metric space.

Proof. 1. It is evident that $d^{(t)}(\mathbf{y}_1, \mathbf{y}_2) \geq 0$ for any $\mathbf{y}_1, \mathbf{y}_2 \in \mathscr{F}^{|In(t)|}$ because the Hamming weight is always nonnegative. Below we will show that $d^{(t)}(\mathbf{y}_1, \mathbf{y}_2) = 0$ if and only if $\mathbf{y}_1 = \mathbf{y}_2$. First, it is easily seen that $d^{(t)}(\mathbf{y}_1, \mathbf{y}_2) = 0$ if $\mathbf{y}_1 = \mathbf{y}_2$. On the other hand, assume that

$$0 = d^{(t)}(\mathbf{y}_1, \mathbf{y}_2) = \min\{w_H(\mathbf{z}) : \mathbf{z} \in \mathscr{F}^{|E|} \text{ such that } \mathbf{y}_1 = \mathbf{y}_2 + \mathbf{z}G_t\},$$

which means that there exists an error vector $\mathbf{z} \in \mathscr{Z}$ with $w_H(\mathbf{z}) = 0$ such that $\mathbf{y}_1 = \mathbf{y}_2 + \mathbf{z}G_t$. Subsequently, $w_H(\mathbf{z}) = 0$ only if $\mathbf{z} = \mathbf{0}$. Thus, $\mathbf{y}_1 = \mathbf{y}_2$.
2. Assume that $d^{(t)}(\mathbf{y}_1, \mathbf{y}_2) = d_1$, that is, there exists an error vector $\mathbf{z} \in \mathscr{F}^{|E|}$ with $w_H(\mathbf{z}) = d_1$ such that $\mathbf{y}_1 = \mathbf{y}_2 + \mathbf{z}G_t$, which is equal to $\mathbf{y}_2 = \mathbf{y}_1 - \mathbf{z}G_t$. Together with the definition of the distance, this implies that

$$d^{(t)}(\mathbf{y}_2, \mathbf{y}_1) \leq w_H(\mathbf{z}) = d_1 = d^{(t)}(\mathbf{y}_1, \mathbf{y}_2).$$

Similarly, we can also obtain

$$d^{(t)}(\mathbf{y}_1, \mathbf{y}_2) \leq d^{(t)}(\mathbf{y}_2, \mathbf{y}_1).$$

Therefore, it follows $d^{(t)}(\mathbf{y}_1, \mathbf{y}_2) = d^{(t)}(\mathbf{y}_2, \mathbf{y}_1)$.

3. Let $d^{(t)}(\mathbf{y}_1,\mathbf{y}_2) = d_{1,2}$, $d^{(t)}(\mathbf{y}_2,\mathbf{y}_3) = d_{2,3}$, and $d^{(t)}(\mathbf{y}_1,\mathbf{y}_3) = d_{1,3}$. Correspondingly, there exist three error vectors $\mathbf{z}_{1,2}, \mathbf{z}_{2,3}, \mathbf{z}_{1,3} \in \mathscr{F}^{|E|}$ with Hamming weight $w_H(\mathbf{z}_{1,2}) = d_{1,2}$, $w_H(\mathbf{z}_{2,3}) = d_{2,3}$, and $w_H(\mathbf{z}_{1,2}) = d_{1,3}$ such that

$$\mathbf{y}_1 = \mathbf{y}_2 + \mathbf{z}_{1,2}G_t, \tag{2.3}$$
$$\mathbf{y}_2 = \mathbf{y}_3 + \mathbf{z}_{2,3}G_t, \tag{2.4}$$
$$\mathbf{y}_1 = \mathbf{y}_3 + \mathbf{z}_{1,3}G_t. \tag{2.5}$$

Combining the equalities (2.3) and (2.4), we have

$$\mathbf{y}_1 = \mathbf{y}_3 + (\mathbf{z}_{1,2} + \mathbf{z}_{2,3})G_t.$$

So it is shown that

$$\begin{aligned}
d_{1,3} &= d^{(t)}(\mathbf{y}_1,\mathbf{y}_3) \\
&= w_H(\mathbf{z}_{1,3}) \\
&\leq w_H(\mathbf{z}_{1,2} + \mathbf{z}_{1,3}) \\
&\leq w_H(\mathbf{z}_{1,2}) + w_H(\mathbf{z}_{1,3}) \\
&= d_{1,2} + d_{2,3}.
\end{aligned}$$

Combining the above (1), (2), and (3), the theorem is proved.   □

Subsequently, we can define the minimum distance of a linear network error correction code at the sink node $t \in T$.

Definition 2.3. The minimum distance of a linear network error correction code at the sink node $t \in T$ is defined as:

$$\begin{aligned}
d_{\min}^{(t)} &= \min\{d^{(t)}(\mathbf{x}_1 F_t, \mathbf{x}_2 F_t) : \text{ all distinct } \mathbf{x}_1, \mathbf{x}_2 \in \mathscr{F}^\omega\} \\
&= \min_{\substack{\mathbf{x}_1, \mathbf{x}_2 \in \mathscr{F}^\omega \\ \mathbf{x}_1 \neq \mathbf{x}_2}} d^{(t)}(\mathbf{x}_1 F_t, \mathbf{x}_2 F_t).
\end{aligned}$$

Intuitively, the weight of an error vector should be a measure of seriousness of the error. So weight measure of an error vector should satisfy the following the conditions at least:

1. The weight measure $w(\cdot)$ for any error vector should be nonnegative, that is, it is a mapping:

$$w: \mathscr{Z} \to \mathbb{Z}^+ \cup \{0\},$$

where $\mathbb{Z}^+$ is the set of all positive integers.
2. For each message vector $\mathbf{x} \in \mathscr{X}$, when $\mathbf{x}$ is transmitted and two distinct error vectors $\mathbf{z}_1$ and $\mathbf{z}_2$ happened respectively, if the two outputs are always the same, these two error vectors should have the same weight.

Actually, it is easy to see that the Hamming weight used in classical coding theory satisfies the two mentioned conditions. Further, recall that in the classical error-correcting coding theory, the Hamming weight can be induced by the Hamming distance, that is, for any $\mathbf{z} \in \mathscr{Z}$, $w_H(\mathbf{z}) = d_H(\mathbf{0}, \mathbf{z})$, where $d_H(\cdot, \cdot)$ represents the Hamming distance. Motivated by this idea, for linear network error correction codes, the distance defined as above should also induce a weight measure for error vectors with respect to each sink node $t \in T$. We state it below.

Definition 2.4. For any error vector $\mathbf{z}$ in $\mathscr{F}^{|E|}$, the weight measure of $\mathbf{z}$ induced by the distance $d^{(t)}(\cdot, \cdot)$ with respect to the sink $t \in T$ is defined as:

$$
\begin{aligned}
w^{(t)}(\mathbf{z}) &= d^{(t)}(\mathbf{0}, \mathbf{z}G_t) \\
&= \min\{w_H(\mathbf{z}') : \text{ all error vectors } \mathbf{z}' \in \mathscr{F}^{|E|} \text{ such that } \mathbf{0} = \mathbf{z}G_t + \mathbf{z}'G_t\} \\
&= \min\{w_H(\mathbf{z}') : \text{ all error vectors } \mathbf{z}' \in \mathscr{F}^{|E|} \text{ such that } \mathbf{z}G_t = \mathbf{z}'G_t\},
\end{aligned}
$$

which is called *network Hamming weight* of the error vector $\mathbf{z}$ with respect to the sink node t.

Now, we will show that this weight of errors satisfies two conditions on weight measure as stated above. First, it is easily to be seen that $w^{(t)}(\mathbf{z})$ is nonnegative for any error vector $\mathbf{z} \in \mathscr{F}^{|E|}$. On the other hand, assume that $\mathbf{z}_1$ and $\mathbf{z}_2$ are arbitrary two error vectors in $\mathscr{F}^{|E|}$ satisfying that, for any message vector $\mathbf{x} \in \mathscr{X}$,

$$
\mathbf{x}F_t + \mathbf{z}_1 G_t = \mathbf{x}F_t + \mathbf{z}_2 G_t,
$$

or equivalently,

$$
\mathbf{z}_1 G_t = \mathbf{z}_2 G_t.
$$

Together with the definition:

$$
w^{(t)}(\mathbf{z}_i) = \min\{w_H(\mathbf{z}') : \text{ all error vectors } \mathbf{z}' \in \mathscr{F}^{|E|} \text{ such that } \mathbf{z}_i G_t = \mathbf{z}'G_t\}, \ i = 1, 2,
$$

it follows $w^{(t)}(\mathbf{z}_1) = w^{(t)}(\mathbf{z}_2)$.

Further, if any two error vectors $\mathbf{z}_1, \mathbf{z}_2 \in \mathscr{F}^{|E|}$ satisfy $\mathbf{z}_1 G_t = \mathbf{z}_2 G_t$, we denote this by $\mathbf{z}_1 \overset{w^{(t)}}{\sim} \mathbf{z}_2$, and then we can obtain the following result easily.

Proposition 2.2. *The relationship* "$\overset{w^{(t)}}{\sim}$" *is an equivalent relation, that is, for any three error vectors* $\mathbf{z}_1, \mathbf{z}_2, \mathbf{z}_3 \in \mathscr{F}^{|E|}$, *it has the following three properties:*

1. $\mathbf{z}_1 \overset{w^{(t)}}{\sim} \mathbf{z}_1$;
2. if $\mathbf{z}_1 \overset{w^{(t)}}{\sim} \mathbf{z}_2$, *then* $\mathbf{z}_2 \overset{w^{(t)}}{\sim} \mathbf{z}_1$;
3. if $\mathbf{z}_1 \overset{w^{(t)}}{\sim} \mathbf{z}_2$, $\mathbf{z}_2 \overset{w^{(t)}}{\sim} \mathbf{z}_3$, *then* $\mathbf{z}_1 \overset{w^{(t)}}{\sim} \mathbf{z}_3$.

In addition, the weight $w^{(t)}(\cdot)$ of error vectors at the sink node $t \in T$ also induces a weight measure for received vectors in vector space $\mathscr{Y}_t = \mathscr{F}^{|In(t)|}$ denoted by $W^{(t)}(\cdot)$. To be specific, let $\mathbf{y} \in \mathscr{Y}_t$ be a received vector at the sink node t, for any error vector $\mathbf{z} \in \mathscr{Z}$ such that $\mathbf{y} = \mathbf{z}G_t$, define:

$$
W^{(t)}(\mathbf{y}) = w^{(t)}(\mathbf{z}).
$$

It is easily seen that $W^{(t)}(\cdot)$ is a mapping from the received message space $\mathscr{Y}_t = \mathscr{F}^{|In(t)|}$ to $\mathbb{Z}^+ \cup \{0\}$. Further, $W^{(t)}(\cdot)$ is well-defined, because the values $w^{(t)}(\mathbf{z})$ for all $\mathbf{z} \in \mathscr{Z}$ satisfying $\mathbf{z}G_t = \mathbf{y}$ are the same from the definition of the weight of errors, and, for any $\mathbf{y} \in \mathscr{Y}_t$, there always exists an error vector $\mathbf{z} \in \mathscr{Z}$ such that $\mathbf{y} = \mathbf{z}G_t$ as G_t is full-rank, i.e., $\text{Rank}(G_t) = |In(t)|$. In other words, for any $\mathbf{y} \in \mathscr{Y}_t$,

$$W^{(t)}(\mathbf{y}) = \min\{w_H(\mathbf{z}) : \mathbf{z} \in \mathscr{Z} \text{ such that } \mathbf{y} = \mathbf{z}G_t\}.$$

In particular, $W^{(t)}(\mathbf{z}G_t) = w^{(t)}(\mathbf{z})$ for any $\mathbf{z} \in \mathscr{Z}$. Then, for any two received vectors $\mathbf{y}_1, \mathbf{y}_2 \in \mathscr{Y}_t$,

$$
\begin{aligned}
d^{(t)}(\mathbf{y}_1, \mathbf{y}_2) &= \min\{w_H(\mathbf{z}) : \mathbf{z} \in \mathscr{Z} \text{ such that } \mathbf{y}_1 = \mathbf{y}_2 + \mathbf{z}G_t\} \\
&= \min\{w_H(\mathbf{z}) : \mathbf{z} \in \mathscr{Z} \text{ such that } \mathbf{y}_1 - \mathbf{y}_2 = \mathbf{z}G_t\} \\
&= W^{(t)}(\mathbf{z}G_t) \\
&= W^{(t)}(\mathbf{y}_1 - \mathbf{y}_2).
\end{aligned}
\tag{2.6}
$$

Particularly, for any two codewords $\mathbf{x}_1 F_t$ and $\mathbf{x}_2 F_t$ at the sink node $t \in T$, we deduce

$$d^{(t)}(\mathbf{x}_1 F_t, \mathbf{x}_2 F_t) = W^{(t)}(\mathbf{x}_1 F_t - \mathbf{x}_2 F_t) = W^{(t)}((\mathbf{x}_1 - \mathbf{x}_2)F_t),$$

which further implies that

$$
\begin{aligned}
d^{(t)}_{\min} &= \min\{d^{(t)}(\mathbf{x}_1 F_t, \mathbf{x}_2 F_t) : \mathbf{x}_1, \mathbf{x}_2 \in \mathscr{X} = \mathscr{F}^\omega \text{ with } \mathbf{x}_1 \neq \mathbf{x}_2\} \\
&= \min\{W^{(t)}((\mathbf{x}_1 - \mathbf{x}_2)F_t) : \mathbf{x}_1, \mathbf{x}_2 \in \mathscr{X} = \mathscr{F}^\omega \text{ with } \mathbf{x}_1 \neq \mathbf{x}_2\} \\
&= \min\{W^{(t)}(\mathbf{x}F_t) : \mathbf{0} \neq \mathbf{x} \in \mathscr{X} = \mathscr{F}^\omega\} \\
&= \min_{\mathbf{x} \in \mathscr{F}^\omega \setminus \{\mathbf{0}\}} W^{(t)}(\mathbf{x}F_t) \\
&= \min_{c \in \mathscr{C}_t \setminus \{\mathbf{0}\}} W^{(t)}(c) \triangleq W^{(t)}(\mathscr{C}_t).
\end{aligned}
\tag{2.7}
$$

$$
\tag{2.8}
$$

We say $W^{(t)}(\mathscr{C}_t)$ the weight of the codebook $\mathscr{C}_t$ with respect to the sink node $t \in T$, which is defined as the minimum weight of all nonzero codewords in $\mathscr{C}_t$.

2.3 Error Correction and Detection Capabilities

In the last section, we have established network error correction model over linear network coding. In this section, we will discuss the error correction and detection capabilities.

Similar to the minimum distance decoding principle for classical error-correcting codes, we can also apply the minimum distance decoding principle to linear network error correction codes at each sink node.

Definition 2.5 (Minimum Distance Decoding Principle). When a vector $\mathbf{y} \in \mathcal{Y}_t$ is received at a sink node $t \in T$, choose a codeword $c \in \mathcal{C}_t$ (or equivalently, $\mathbf{x}F_t \in \mathcal{C}_t$) that is closest to the received vector $\mathbf{y}$. To be specific, choose a codeword $c \in \mathcal{C}_t$ (or equivalently, $\mathbf{x}F_t \in \mathcal{C}_t$) such that

$$d^{(t)}(\mathbf{y},c) = \min_{c' \in \mathcal{C}_t} d^{(t)}(\mathbf{y},c')$$
$$= \min_{\mathbf{x} \in \mathcal{F}^\omega} d^{(t)}(\mathbf{y},\mathbf{x}F_t).$$

And refer to this as the *minimum distance decoding principle* at the sink node $t \in T$.

Definition 2.6 (d-Error-Detecting). Let d be a positive integer. A linear network error correction code is d-error-detecting at the sink node $t \in T$, if, whichever error vector $\mathbf{z} \in \mathcal{Z}$ with weight $w^{(t)}(\mathbf{z})$ no more than d but at least one happens, when any source message vector in $\mathcal{X}$ is transmitted by this linear network error correction code, the received vector at the sink node t is not a codeword. A linear network error correction code is exactly d-error-detecting at the sink node $t \in T$, if it is d-error-detecting but not $(d+1)$-error-detecting at t.

Definition 2.7 (d-Error-Correcting). Let d be a positive integer. A linear network error correction code is d-error-correcting at the sink node $t \in T$, if the minimum distance decoding principle at the sink node t is able to correct any error vector in $\mathcal{Z}$ with weight no more than d, assuming that the incomplete decoding[1] rule is used. A linear network error correction code is exactly d-error-correcting at the sink node t if it is d-error-correcting but not $(d+1)$-error-correcting at t.

In the following two theorems, it is shown that, similar to classical coding theory, the error detection and error correction capabilities of linear network error correction codes at each sink node are characterized by its corresponding minimum distance.

Theorem 2.2. *A linear network error correction code is exactly d-error-detecting at sink node t, if and only if $d_{\min}^{(t)} = d + 1$.*

Proof. First, assume that $d_{\min}^{(t)} = d + 1$. Then we claim that this linear network error correction code is d-error-detecting at the sink node t, that is, for any message vector $\mathbf{x}_1 \in \mathcal{F}^\omega$ and any error vector $\mathbf{z} \in \mathcal{F}^{|E|}$ with $1 \le w^{(t)}(\mathbf{z}) \le d$,

$$\mathbf{x}_1 F_t + \mathbf{z}G_t \notin \mathcal{C}_t = \{\mathbf{x}F_t : \text{ all } \mathbf{x} \in \mathcal{F}^\omega\}.$$

On the contrary, suppose that there exists some message vector $\mathbf{x}_1 \in \mathcal{F}^\omega$ and some error vector $\mathbf{z} \in \mathcal{F}^{|E|}$ with $1 \le w^{(t)}(\mathbf{z}) \le d$ such that

$$\mathbf{x}_1 F_t + \mathbf{z}G_t \in \mathcal{C}_t,$$

---

[1] Incomplete decoding refers to the case that if a word is received, find the closest codeword. If there are more than one such codewords, request a retransmission. The counterpart is complete decoding which means that if there are more than one such codewords, select one of them arbitrarily.

which means that there exists another message vector $\mathbf{x}_2 \in \mathscr{F}^\omega$ such that

$$\mathbf{x}_1 F_t + \mathbf{z} G_t = \mathbf{x}_2 F_t.$$

Together with the equality (2.6), this implies that

$$d^{(t)}(\mathbf{x}_1 F_t, \mathbf{x}_2 F_t) = W^{(t)}(\mathbf{x}_1 F_t - \mathbf{x}_2 F_t) = W^{(t)}(\mathbf{z} G_t) = w^{(t)}(\mathbf{z}) \le d,$$

which contradicts to $d_{\min}^{(t)} = d+1 > d$.

In the following, we will show that this linear network error correction code is not $(d+1)$-error-detecting at t. Since $d_{\min}^{(t)} = d+1$, then there exist two codewords $\mathbf{x}_1 F_t$ and $\mathbf{x}_2 F_t$ satisfying

$$d^{(t)}(\mathbf{x}_1 F_t, \mathbf{x}_2 F_t) = d+1.$$

That is, there exists an error vector $\mathbf{z}$ with $w^{(t)}(\mathbf{z}) = d+1$ such that $\mathbf{x}_1 F_t = \mathbf{x}_2 F_t + \mathbf{z} G_t$, which indicates that this linear network error correction code is not $(d+1)$-error-detecting code at the sink node $t \in T$.

On the other hand, let this linear network error correction code be exactly d-error-detecting at the sink node $t \in T$. To be specific, it is d-error-detecting and not $(d+1)$-error-detecting at t. The d-error-detecting property shows $\mathbf{x} F_t + \mathbf{z} G_t \notin \mathscr{C}_t$ for any codeword $\mathbf{x} F_t \in \mathscr{C}_t$ and any error vector $\mathbf{z} \in \mathscr{L}$ with $1 \le w^{(t)}(\mathbf{z}) \le d$. Thus, it follows $d_{\min}^{(t)} \ge d+1$.

Conversely, assume that $d_{\min}^{(t)} < d+1$. Notice that $d_{\min}^{(t)} = \min_{\mathbf{x} \in \mathscr{F}^\omega \setminus \{0\}} W^{(t)}(\mathbf{x} F_t)$ from (2.7), which implies that there is a codeword $\mathbf{x}_1 F_t \in \mathscr{C}_t$ satisfying $W^{(t)}(\mathbf{x}_1 F_t) = d_{\min}^{(t)} < d+1$. Further, let $\mathbf{z} \in \mathscr{L}$ be an error vector satisfying $\mathbf{x}_1 F_t = \mathbf{z} G_t$, and thus one has

$$1 \le w^{(t)}(\mathbf{z}) = W^{(t)}(\mathbf{z} G_t) = W^{(t)}(\mathbf{x}_1 F_t) = d_{\min}^{(t)} < d+1.$$

Thus, for any codeword $\mathbf{x}_2 F_t \in \mathscr{C}_t$, we have

$$\mathbf{x}_2 F_t + \mathbf{z} G_t = \mathbf{x}_2 F_t + \mathbf{x}_1 F_t = (\mathbf{x}_1 + \mathbf{x}_2) F_t \in \mathscr{C}_t,$$

which, together with $1 \le w^{(t)}(\mathbf{z}) \le d$, violates the d-error-detecting property at the sink node t. In addition, this LNEC code is not $(d+1)$-error-detecting at the sink node t, that is, there exists a codeword $\mathbf{x} F_t \in \mathscr{C}_t$ and an error vector $\mathbf{z} \in \mathscr{F}^{|E|}$ with $w^{(t)}(\mathbf{z}) = d+1$ such that $\mathbf{x} F_t + \mathbf{z} G_t \in \mathscr{C}_t$. Let $\mathbf{x}_1 F_t = \mathbf{x} F_t + \mathbf{z} G_t$ for some $\mathbf{x}_1 \in \mathscr{F}^\omega$, and then

$$d_{\min}^{(t)} \le d^{(t)}(\mathbf{x}_1 F_t, \mathbf{x} F_t) = W^{(t)}(\mathbf{x}_1 F_t - \mathbf{x} F_t) = W^{(t)}(\mathbf{z} G_t) = w^{(t)}(\mathbf{z}) = d+1.$$

Combining the above, it is shown $d_{\min}^{(t)} = d+1$. This completes the proof. $\qquad \square$

Theorem 2.3. *A linear network error correction code is exactly d-error-correcting at sink node t if and only if $d_{\min}^{(t)} = 2d+1$ or $d_{\min}^{(t)} = 2d+2$.*

Proof. First, we assume that a linear network error correction code is d-error-correcting at the sink node $t \in T$, which means that, for any codeword $\mathbf{x}F_t \in \mathscr{C}_t$ and any error vector $\mathbf{z} \in \mathscr{Z}$ with weight no more than d, it follows

$$d^{(t)}(\mathbf{x}F_t, \mathbf{x}F_t + \mathbf{z}G_t) < d^{(t)}(\mathbf{x}'F_t, \mathbf{x}F_t + \mathbf{z}G_t),$$

for any other codeword $\mathbf{x}'F_t \in \mathscr{C}_t$.

We will show that $d_{\min}^{(t)} > 2d$ below. Assume the contrary that $d_{\min}^{(t)} \leq 2d$, that is, there exist two distinct codewords $\mathbf{x}_1 F_t, \mathbf{x}_2 F_t \in \mathscr{C}_t$ satisfying

$$d^{(t)}(\mathbf{x}_1 F_t, \mathbf{x}_2 F_t) \leq 2d.$$

Subsequently, we can always choose an error vector $\mathbf{z} \in \mathscr{Z}$ such that $\mathbf{x}_1 F_t - \mathbf{x}_2 F_t = \mathbf{z}G_t$ from $A_{In(t)}G_t = I_{|In(t)|}$ where again $I_{|In(t)|}$ is an $|In(t)| \times |In(t)|$ identity matrix. Thus, one has

$$2d \geq d^{(t)}(\mathbf{x}_1 F_t, \mathbf{x}_2 F_t) = W^{(t)}(\mathbf{x}_1 F_t - \mathbf{x}_2 F_t) = W^{(t)}(\mathbf{z}G_t) = w^{(t)}(\mathbf{z}) \triangleq \hat{d}.$$

Note that $w^{(t)}(\mathbf{z}) = \min\{w_H(\mathbf{z}') : \text{all } \mathbf{z}' \in \mathscr{Z} \text{ such that } \mathbf{z}G_t = \mathbf{z}'G_t\}$. Thus, without loss of generality, we assume that

$$w^{(t)}(\mathbf{z}) = w_H(\mathbf{z}).$$

Further, let $d_1 = \lceil \frac{\hat{d}-1}{2} \rceil$ and $d_2 = \lfloor \frac{\hat{d}+1}{2} \rfloor$. And it is not difficult to see that

$$d_1 \leq d_2 \leq d \text{ and } d_1 + d_2 = \hat{d}.$$

Thus, we can claim that, there exist two error vectors $\mathbf{z}_1, \mathbf{z}_2 \in \mathscr{Z}$ satisfying:

- $w_H(\mathbf{z}_1) = d_1$ and $w_H(\mathbf{z}_2) = d_2$, respectively;
- $\rho_{\mathbf{z}_1} \cap \rho_{\mathbf{z}_2} = \emptyset$ and $\rho_{\mathbf{z}_1} \cup \rho_{\mathbf{z}_2} = \rho_{\mathbf{z}}$;
- $\mathbf{z} = \mathbf{z}_1 + \mathbf{z}_2$;

where $\rho_{\mathbf{z}'}$ is called an error pattern induced by an error vector $\mathbf{z}' \in \mathscr{Z}$, defined as the set of the channels on which the corresponding coordinates of $\mathbf{z}'$ are nonzero. Below, we will indicate that

$$w_H(\mathbf{z}_i) = w^{(t)}(\mathbf{z}_i), \ i = 1, 2.$$

Clearly, we know $w^{(t)}(\mathbf{z}_1) \leq w_H(\mathbf{z}_1)$. Further, if $w^{(t)}(\mathbf{z}_1) < w_H(\mathbf{z}_1)$, there exists an error vector $\mathbf{z}_1' \in \mathscr{Z}$ satisfying $\mathbf{z}_1' G_t = \mathbf{z}_1 G_t$ and

$$w_H(\mathbf{z}_1') = w^{(t)}(\mathbf{z}_1') = w^{(t)}(\mathbf{z}_1) < w_H(\mathbf{z}_1). \tag{2.9}$$

Thus, we have

$$(\mathbf{z}_1' + \mathbf{z}_2)G_t = \mathbf{z}_1' G_t + \mathbf{z}_2 G_t = \mathbf{z}_1 G_t + \mathbf{z}_2 G_t = (\mathbf{z}_1 + \mathbf{z}_2)G_t = \mathbf{z}G_t,$$

which leads to

$$w_H(\mathbf{z}_1' + \mathbf{z}_2) \leq w_H(\mathbf{z}_1') + w_H(\mathbf{z}_2)$$
$$< w_H(\mathbf{z}_1) + w_H(\mathbf{z}_2) \tag{2.10}$$
$$= w_H(\mathbf{z}_1 + \mathbf{z}_2) \tag{2.11}$$
$$= w_H(\mathbf{z})$$
$$= w^{(t)}(\mathbf{z}),$$

where the inequality (2.10) follows from (2.9) and the equality (2.11) follows from $\rho_{\mathbf{z}_1} \cap \rho_{\mathbf{z}_2} = \emptyset$. This means that there exists an error vector $\mathbf{z}_1' + \mathbf{z}_2 \in \mathscr{Z}$ satisfying $(\mathbf{z}_1' + \mathbf{z}_2)G_t = \mathbf{z}G_t$ and $w_H(\mathbf{z}_1' + \mathbf{z}_2) < w^{(t)}(\mathbf{z})$, which evidently violates the fact that

$$w^{(t)}(\mathbf{z}) = \min\{w_H(\mathbf{z}') : \text{ all } \mathbf{z}' \in \mathscr{Z} \text{ such that } \mathbf{z}'G_t = \mathbf{z}G_t\}.$$

Therefore, one obtains $w_H(\mathbf{z}_1) = w^{(t)}(\mathbf{z}_1)$. Similarly, we can also deduce $w_H(\mathbf{z}_2) = w^{(t)}(\mathbf{z}_2)$.

Combining the above, we have

$$\mathbf{x}_1 F_t - \mathbf{x}_2 F_t = \mathbf{z}G_t = \mathbf{z}_1 G_t + \mathbf{z}_2 G_t,$$

subsequently,

$$\mathbf{x}_1 F_t - \mathbf{z}_1 G_t = \mathbf{x}_2 F_t + \mathbf{z}_2 G_t.$$

This implies that

$$d^{(t)}(\mathbf{x}_1 F_t, \mathbf{x}_2 F_t \mid \mathbf{z}_2 G_t) = d^{(t)}(\mathbf{x}_1 F_t, \mathbf{x}_1 F_t - \mathbf{z}_1 G_t)$$
$$= W^{(t)}(\mathbf{z}_1 G_t) = w^{(t)}(\mathbf{z}_1) = w_H(\mathbf{z}_1) = d_1$$
$$\leq d_2 = w_H(\mathbf{z}_2) = w^{(t)}(\mathbf{z}_2) = W^{(t)}(\mathbf{z}_2 G_t)$$
$$= d^{(t)}(\mathbf{x}_2 F_t, \mathbf{x}_2 F_t + \mathbf{z}_2 G_t),$$

which further implies that when the message vector $\mathbf{x}_2$ is transmitted and the error vector $\mathbf{z}_2$ happens, the minimum distance decoding principle can not decode $\mathbf{x}_2$ successfully at the sink node t. This is a contradiction to d-error-correcting property at the sink node $t \in T$. So the hypothesis is not true, which indicates $d_{\min}^{(t)} \geq 2d + 1$.

On the other hand, if this LNEC code is not $(d+1)$-error-correcting, then $d_{\min}^{(t)} \leq 2d+2$. Conversely, suppose that $d_{\min}^{(t)} \geq 2d+3$. We know that the fact that this LNEC code is not $(d+1)$-error-correcting at the sink node $t \in T$ means that there exists a codeword $\mathbf{x}_1 F_t \in \mathscr{C}_t$ and an error vector $\mathbf{z}_1 \in \mathscr{Z}$ with $w^{(t)}(\mathbf{z}_1) = d+1$ such that when the message vector $\mathbf{x}_1$ is transmitted and the error vector $\mathbf{z}_1$ happens, the minimum distance decoding principle cannot decode $\mathbf{x}_1$ successfully at the sink node t. To be specific, there exists another message $\mathbf{x}_2 \in \mathscr{X}$ satisfying:

$$d^{(t)}(\mathbf{x}_2 F_t, \mathbf{x}_1 F_t + \mathbf{z}_1 G_t) \leq d^{(t)}(\mathbf{x}_1 F_t, \mathbf{x}_1 F_t + \mathbf{z}_1 G_t),$$

that is, there exists an error vector $\mathbf{z}_2 \in \mathscr{Z}$ with $w^{(t)}(\mathbf{z}_2) \leq d+1$ satisfying

$$\mathbf{x}_2 F_t + \mathbf{z}_2 G_t = \mathbf{x}_1 F_t + \mathbf{z}_1 G_t.$$

Therefore,

$$
\begin{aligned}
d^{(t)}(\mathbf{x}_1 F_t, \mathbf{x}_2 F_t) &\leq d^{(t)}(\mathbf{x}_1 F_t, \mathbf{x}_1 F_t + \mathbf{z}_1 G_t) + d^{(t)}(\mathbf{x}_2 F_t, \mathbf{x}_2 F_t + \mathbf{z}_2 G_t) \\
&= W^{(t)}(\mathbf{z}_1 G_t) + W^{(t)}(\mathbf{z}_2 G_t) \\
&= w^{(t)}(\mathbf{z}_1) + w^{(t)}(\mathbf{z}_2) \\
&\leq 2d + 2,
\end{aligned}
$$

which violates $d_{\min}^{(t)} \geq 2d+3$. Therefore, combining two cases $d_{\min}^{(t)} \geq 2d+1$ and $d_{\min}^{(t)} \leq 2d+2$, we obtain $d_{\min}^{(t)} = 2d+1$, or $2d+2$.

In the following, we prove the sufficiency of the theorem. First, we consider the case $d_{\min}^{(t)} = 2d+1$. For this case, this LNEC code is d-error-correcting at the sink node $t \in T$, that is, for any codeword $\mathbf{x} F_t \in \mathscr{C}_t$ and any error vector $\mathbf{z} \in \mathscr{Z}$ with weight no more than d, it follows

$$d^{(t)}(\mathbf{x} F_t, \mathbf{x} F_t + \mathbf{z} G_t) < d^{(t)}(\mathbf{x}' F_t, \mathbf{x} F_t + \mathbf{z} G_t),$$

for any other codeword $\mathbf{x}' F_t \in \mathscr{C}_t$.

Assume the contrary that there are two distinct codewords $\mathbf{x}_1 F_t, \mathbf{x}_2 F_t \in \mathscr{C}_t$ and an error vector $\mathbf{z} \in \mathscr{Z}$ with weight no more than d such that

$$d^{(t)}(\mathbf{x}_2 F_t, \mathbf{x}_1 F_t + \mathbf{z} G_t) \leq d^{(t)}(\mathbf{x}_1 F_t, \mathbf{x}_1 F_t + \mathbf{z} G_t).$$

Therefore, we have

$$
\begin{aligned}
d^{(t)}(\mathbf{x}_1 F_t, \mathbf{x}_2 F_t) &\leq d^{(t)}(\mathbf{x}_1 F_t, \mathbf{x}_1 F_t + \mathbf{z} G_t) + d^{(t)}(\mathbf{x}_2 F_t, \mathbf{x}_1 F_t + \mathbf{z} G_t) \\
&\leq 2d^{(t)}(\mathbf{x}_1 F_t, \mathbf{x}_1 F_t + \mathbf{z} G_t) \\
&= 2W^{(t)}(\mathbf{z} G_t) \\
&= 2w^{(t)}(\mathbf{z}) \\
&\leq 2d,
\end{aligned}
$$

which contradicts to $d_{\min}^{(t)} = 2d+1$.

On the other hand, this LNEC code is not $(d+1)$-error-correcting at the sink node $t \in T$. As $d_{\min}^{(t)} = 2d+1$, there exist two codewords $\mathbf{x}_1 F_t, \mathbf{x}_2 F_t \in \mathscr{C}_t$ such that

$$d^{(t)}(\mathbf{x}_1 F_t, \mathbf{x}_2 F_t) = 2d+1,$$

which further shows that there exists an error vector $\mathbf{z} \in \mathscr{Z}$ with $w^{(t)}(\mathbf{z}) = 2d+1$ such that

$$\mathbf{x}_1 F_t = \mathbf{x}_2 F_t + \mathbf{z} G_t. \tag{2.12}$$

Together with the definition of weight

$$w^{(t)}(\mathbf{z}) = \min\{w_H(\mathbf{z}') : \text{ all } \mathbf{z}' \in \mathscr{Z} \text{ such that } \mathbf{z}'G_t = \mathbf{z}G_t\},$$

without loss of generality, we assume $\mathbf{z} \in \mathscr{Z}$ satisfying $w_H(\mathbf{z}) = w^{(t)}(\mathbf{z}) = 2d + 1$.

Subsequently, let $\mathbf{z}_1, \mathbf{z}_2 \in \mathscr{Z}$ be two error vectors satisfying $\mathbf{z} = \mathbf{z}_1 + \mathbf{z}_2$ with the following two conditions:

- $\rho_{\mathbf{z}_1} \cap \rho_{\mathbf{z}_2} = \emptyset$ and $\rho_{\mathbf{z}_1} \cup \rho_{\mathbf{z}_2} = \rho_{\mathbf{z}}$;
- $|\rho_{\mathbf{z}_1}| = d$, and $|\rho_{\mathbf{z}_2}| = d + 1$.

Now, we can claim that $w_H(\mathbf{z}_1) = w^{(t)}(\mathbf{z}_1) = d$ and $w_H(\mathbf{z}_2) = w^{(t)}(\mathbf{z}_2) = d + 1$. On the contrary, assume that $w_H(\mathbf{z}_1) \neq w^{(t)}(\mathbf{z}_1)$, which, together with $w_H(\mathbf{z}_1) \geq w^{(t)}(\mathbf{z}_1)$, indicates $w_H(\mathbf{z}_1) > w^{(t)}(\mathbf{z}_1)$. Again notice that

$$w^{(t)}(\mathbf{z}_1) = \min\{w_H(\mathbf{z}_1') : \text{ all } \mathbf{z}_1' \in \mathscr{Z} \text{ such that } \mathbf{z}_1'G_t = \mathbf{z}_1G_t\}.$$

It follows that there must exist an error vector $\mathbf{z}_1' \in \mathscr{Z}$ such that $w_H(\mathbf{z}_1') = w^{(t)}(\mathbf{z}_1)$ and $\mathbf{z}_1'G_t = \mathbf{z}_1G_t$. Thus, it is shown that

$$(\mathbf{z}_1' + \mathbf{z}_2)G_t = \mathbf{z}_1'G_t + \mathbf{z}_2G_t = \mathbf{z}_1G_t + \mathbf{z}_2G_t = \mathbf{z}G_t,$$

which implies that $w^{(t)}(\mathbf{z}_1' + \mathbf{z}_2) = w^{(t)}(\mathbf{z})$. However,

$$
\begin{aligned}
w_H(\mathbf{z}_1' + \mathbf{z}_2) &\leq w_H(\mathbf{z}_1') + w_H(\mathbf{z}_2) \\
&= w^{(t)}(\mathbf{z}_1) + w_H(\mathbf{z}_2) \\
&< w_H(\mathbf{z}_1) + w_H(\mathbf{z}_2) \\
&= w_H(\mathbf{z}_1 + \mathbf{z}_2) \\
&= w_H(\mathbf{z}) \\
&= w^{(t)}(\mathbf{z}) \\
&= w^{(t)}(\mathbf{z}_1' + \mathbf{z}_2),
\end{aligned}
$$

which is impossible. Similarly, we can also obtain $w_H(\mathbf{z}_2) = w^{(t)}(\mathbf{z}_2) = d + 1$. Therefore, from (2.12), one has

$$\mathbf{x}_1F_t = \mathbf{x}_2F_t + \mathbf{z}G_t = \mathbf{x}_2F_t + \mathbf{z}_1G_t + \mathbf{z}_2G_t,$$

that is,

$$\mathbf{x}_1F_t - \mathbf{z}_1G_t = \mathbf{x}_2F_t + \mathbf{z}_2G_t.$$

So when the message vector $\mathbf{x}_2$ is transmitted and the error vector $\mathbf{z}_2$ happens, the minimum distance decoding principle cannot decode $\mathbf{x}_2$ successfully at the sink node t, that is, it is not $(d+1)$-error-correcting at the sink node $t \in T$.

Combining the above, this LNEC code is exactly d-error-correcting at the sink node $t \in T$. Similarly, we can show that $d_{\min}^{(t)} = 2d + 2$ also implies exactly d-error-correcting at the sink node $t \in T$. The proof is completed. □

Corollary 2.1. *For a linear network error correction code, $d_{\min}^{(t)} = d$ if and only if it is exactly $\lfloor \frac{d-1}{2} \rfloor$-error-correcting at the sink node $t \in T$.*

Remark 2.1. In [51], the authors indicated an interesting discovery that, for nonlinear network error correction codes, the number of the correctable errors can be more than half of the number of the detectable errors, which is contrast to the linear cases as stated above.

In classical coding theory, if the positions of errors occurred are known by the decoder, the errors are called erasure errors. When network coding is under consideration, this scheme can be extended to linear network error correction codes. To be specific, we assume that the collection of channels on which errors may be occurred during the network transmission is known by sink nodes. For this case, we will characterize the capability for correcting erasure errors with respect to sink nodes, that is called *erasure error correction capability*. This characterization is a generalization of the corresponding result in classical coding theory.

Let ρ be an error pattern consisting of the channels on which errors may happen, and we say that an error message vector $\mathbf{z} = [z_e : e \in E]$ matches an error pattern ρ, if $z_e = 0$ for all $e \in E \backslash \rho$. Since the error pattern ρ is known by the sink nodes, a weight measure $w^{(t)}$ of the error pattern ρ with respect to the weight measure $w^{(t)}$ of error vectors at the sink node t is defined as:

$$w^{(t)}(\rho) \triangleq \max_{\mathbf{z} \in \mathscr{Z}_\rho} w^{(t)}(\mathbf{z}),$$

where $\mathscr{Z}_\rho$ represents the collection of all error vectors matching the error pattern ρ, i.e.,

$$\mathscr{Z}_\rho = \{ \mathbf{z} : \mathbf{z} \in \mathscr{F}^{|E|} \text{ and } \mathbf{z} \text{ matches } \rho \}.$$

Naturally, we still use the minimum distance decoding principle to correct erasure errors at sink nodes. First, we give the following definition.

Definition 2.8 (d-Erasure-Error-Correcting). Let d be a positive integer. A linear network error correction code is d-erasure-error-correcting at the sink node $t \in T$, if the minimum distance decoding principle at the sink node t is able to correct all error vectors in $\mathscr{Z}$ matching any error pattern ρ with weight no more than d, assuming that ρ is known by t and the incomplete decoding rule is used.

The following result characterizes the erasure error correction capability of linear network error correction codes.

Theorem 2.4. *A linear network error correction code is d-erasure-error-correcting at the sink node $t \in T$ if and only if $d_{\min}^{(t)} \geq d + 1$.*

Proof. First, we prove that $d_{\min}^{(t)} \geq d+1$ is a sufficient condition. Assume that $d_{\min}^{(t)} \geq d+1$, and the contrary that this linear network error correction code is not d-erasure-error-correcting at the sink node t. That is, for some error pattern ρ with weight no more than d with respect to t, there are two distinct message vectors $\mathbf{x}_1, \mathbf{x}_2 \in \mathscr{F}^\omega$ and two distinct error vectors $\mathbf{z}_1, \mathbf{z}_2$ matching the error pattern ρ (or equivalently, $\mathbf{z}_1, \mathbf{z}_2 \in \mathscr{Z}_\rho$) such that

$$\mathbf{x}_1 F_t + \mathbf{z}_1 G_t = \mathbf{x}_2 F_t + \mathbf{z}_2 G_t.$$

Subsequently,

$$\mathbf{x}_1 F_t - \mathbf{x}_2 F_t = \mathbf{z}_2 G_t - \mathbf{z}_1 G_t,$$

which further shows

$$d^{(t)}(\mathbf{x}_1 F_t, \mathbf{x}_2 F_t) = W^{(t)}((\mathbf{z}_2 - \mathbf{z}_1)G_t) = w^{(t)}(\mathbf{z}_2 - \mathbf{z}_1) \leq w^{(t)}(\rho) \leq d, \qquad (2.13)$$

where the first inequality in (2.13) follows from both $\mathbf{z}_1$ and $\mathbf{z}_2$ matching ρ. This violates $d_{\min}^{(t)} \geq d+1$.

On the other hand, we will prove the necessary condition of this theorem by contradiction. Assume a linear network error correction code has $d_{\min}^{(t)} \leq d$ for some sink node t. We will find an error pattern ρ with weight $w^{(t)}(\rho) \leq d$ which can not be corrected.

Since $d_{\min}^{(t)} \leq d$, there exist two codewords $\mathbf{x}_1 F_t, \mathbf{x}_2 F_t \in \mathscr{C}_t$ such that

$$d^{(t)}(\mathbf{x}_1 F_t, \mathbf{x}_2 F_t) \leq d.$$

Further, there exists an error vector $\mathbf{z} \in \mathscr{Z}$ such that $\mathbf{x}_1 F_t - \mathbf{x}_2 F_t = \mathbf{z} G_t$ and

$$w^{(t)}(\mathbf{z}) = W^{(t)}(\mathbf{z} G_t) = W^{(t)}(\mathbf{x}_1 F_t - \mathbf{x}_2 F_t) = d^{(t)}(\mathbf{x}_1 F_t, \mathbf{x}_2 F_t) \leq d.$$

Note that
$$w^{(t)}(\mathbf{z}) = \min\{w_H(\mathbf{z}') : \mathbf{z}' \in \mathscr{Z} \text{ such that } \mathbf{z}' G_t = \mathbf{z} G_t\}.$$

Without loss of generality, assume the error vector $\mathbf{z}$ satisfying $w_H(\mathbf{z}) = w^{(t)}(\mathbf{z}) \leq d$. Let $\rho_{\mathbf{z}}$ further be the error pattern induced by the error vector $\mathbf{z}$, that is the collection of channels on which the corresponding coordinates of $\mathbf{z}$ are nonzero. Hence,

$$w^{(t)}(\rho_{\mathbf{z}}) \leq |\rho_{\mathbf{z}}| = w_H(\mathbf{z}) \leq d.$$

This shows that when the message vector $\mathbf{x}_2$ is transmitted and the erasure error vector $\mathbf{z}$ matching ρ with $w^{(t)}(\rho) \leq d$ happens, the minimum distance decoding principle at the sink node t will decode $\mathbf{x}_1$ instead of $\mathbf{x}_2$, that is, $\mathbf{x}_2$ can not be decoded successfully at the sink node t, although ρ is known. This leads to a contradiction.

Combining the above, we complete the proof. $\qquad \qquad \square$

Chapter 3
Another Description of Linear Network Error Correction Model

We have established linear network error correction model in the last chapter. In this chapter, we will introduce another equivalent description of linear network error correction model so as to facilitate important and interesting problems in linear network error correction coding such as encoding, decoding, the analysis and the constructions of linear network error correction codes, etc. Actually, this description is a local approach to represent linear network error correction coding process and it will be discussed in more detail in the chapter.

3.1 Local Description of Linear Network Error Correction Model

Similar to linear network codes, we can still define local description and global description for linear network error correction codes. In this case, we also treat the errors as messages that is called *error messages*. A local approach can be introduced to represent the linear network error correction coding process. First, we introduce the extended network as follows. In the original network $G = (V, E)$, for each channel $e \in E$, an imaginary channel e' is introduced, which is connected to the tail of e to provide error message. Define a new network $\tilde{G}$ including the original network G and all imaginary channels, say the extended network of G. Specifically, let $\tilde{G} = (\tilde{V}, \tilde{E})$, where $\tilde{V} = V$ and $\tilde{E} = E \cup E' \cup \{d_1', d_2', \cdots, d_\omega'\}$ with $E' = \{e' : e \in E\}$. Obviously, $|E'| = |E|$. Then a linear network code for the original network can be extended to a linear network code for the extended network by letting $k_{e',e} = 1$ and $k_{e',d} = 0$ for all $d \in E \setminus \{e\}$. For each internal node i in the extended network $\tilde{G}$, note that $In(i)$ only includes the real incoming channels of i, that is, the imaginary channels e' corresponding to $e \in Out(i)$ are not in $In(i)$. But for the source node s, we still define $In(s) = \{d_1', d_2', \cdots, d_\omega'\}$. In order to distinguish two different types of imaginary channels, we say d_i' for $1 \leq i \leq \omega$ the *imaginary message channels* and e'

X. Guang and Z. Zhang, *Linear Network Error Correction Coding*, SpringerBriefs in Computer Science, DOI 10.1007/978-1-4939-0588-1_3, © The Author(s) 2014

for $e \in E$ the *imaginary error channels*.[1] We can also define global encoding kernel $\tilde{f}_e$ for each $e \in \tilde{E}$ in the extended network. It is an $(\omega + |E|)$-dimensional column vector and the entries can be indexed by all channels in $In(s) \cup E$. For imaginary message channels d'_i, $1 \leq i \leq \omega$, and imaginary error channels $e' \in E'$, let $\tilde{f}_{d'_i} = 1_{d'_i}$, $\tilde{f}_{e'} = 1_e$, where 1_d is an $(\omega + |E|)$-dimensional column vector which is the indicator function of $d \in In(s) \cup E$. Thus, the vectors $\tilde{f}_e$ for both ω imaginary message channels and $|E|$ imaginary error channels form the standard basis of vector space $\mathscr{F}^{\omega + |E|}$. For other global encoding kernels $\tilde{f}_e, e \in E$, we have recursive formulae:

$$\tilde{f}_e = \sum_{d \in In(tail(e))} k_{d,e} \tilde{f}_d + 1_e.$$

We say $\tilde{f}_e$ the extended global encoding kernel of the channel e for the original network.

From extended global encoding kernels, for a channel $e \in E$ on which there is no error, it follows

$$(\mathbf{x}\,\mathbf{z}) \cdot \tilde{f}_e = (\mathbf{x}\,\mathbf{z}) \cdot (\tilde{f}_e - 1_e) = U_e = \tilde{U}_e,$$

and, if there is an error $z_e \neq 0$ on channel e, then

$$(\mathbf{x}\,\mathbf{z}) \cdot \tilde{f}_e = (\mathbf{x}\,\mathbf{z}) \cdot (\tilde{f}_e - 1_e) + z_e = U_e + z_e = \tilde{U}_e,$$

where review that $\tilde{U}_e$ is the output of the channel e, U_e is the message that should be transmitted on the channel e and z_e is the error occurred on e. Furthermore, similar to the Koetter-Médard Formula (1.1), there also exists a formula [59]:

$$[\tilde{f}_e : e \in E] = \begin{bmatrix} B \\ I \end{bmatrix} (I - K)^{-1}. \tag{3.1}$$

where I is an $|E| \times |E|$ identity matrix.

At a sink node t, the messages $\{\tilde{U}_e : e \in In(t)\}$ and the extended global encoding kernels $\{\tilde{f}_e : e \in In(t)\}$ are available. The matrix

$$\tilde{F}_t = [\tilde{f}_e : e \in In(t)]$$

is also called the *decoding matrix* at the sink node $t \in T$. And note that

---

[1] In order to facilitate our discussion, we assume that all imaginary message channels and imaginary error channels have no tail nodes. Actually, we can take for granted that there is an auxiliary node s' as the tail node for all imaginary message channels, i.e., s' generates all source messages, and similarly, there is another auxiliary node s^* as the tail node for all imaginary error channels, i.e., s^* generates all error messages. Particularly, s' and s^* are allowed to be the same one.

$$\tilde{F}_t = \left[\tilde{f}_e : e \in In(t)\right]$$
$$= \left[\tilde{f}_e : e \in E\right] A_{In(t)}^\top$$
$$= \begin{bmatrix} B \\ I \end{bmatrix} (I-K)^{-1} A_{In(t)}^\top$$
$$= \begin{bmatrix} B(I-K)^{-1} A_{In(t)}^\top \\ (I-K)^{-1} A_{In(t)}^\top \end{bmatrix}$$
$$= \begin{bmatrix} F_t \\ G_t \end{bmatrix}.$$

Let further the received vector at the sink node t be

$$\mathbf{y} = \left(\tilde{U}_e : e \in In(t)\right).$$

Then, the equation

$$\mathbf{y} = (\mathbf{x}\,\mathbf{z}) \cdot \tilde{F}_t = (\mathbf{x}\,\mathbf{z}) \cdot \begin{bmatrix} F_t \\ G_t \end{bmatrix} = \mathbf{x}F_t + \mathbf{z}G_t \tag{3.2}$$

is called the decoding equation of a linear network error correction code at the sink node t. Note that this decoding equation is the same as Eq. (2.2) we have discussed in Chap. 2.

Similar to linear network codes, we can also define a linear network error correction code by either a local description or a global description.

Definition 3.1.

Local Description of a Linear Network Error Correction Code. An ω-dimen sional $\mathscr{F}$-valued linear network error correction code consists of all local encoding kernels at internal nodes (including the source node s), i.e.,

$$K = (k_{d,e})_{d \in In(i), e \in Out(i)},$$

that is an $|In(i)| \times |Out(i)|$ matrix for the node i, where $k_{d,e} \in \mathscr{F}$ is the local encoding coefficient for the adjacent pair (d,e) of channels with $d \in In(i)$, $e \in Out(i)$.

Global Description of a Linear Network Error Correction Code. An ω-dimen sional $\mathscr{F}$-valued linear network error correction code consists of all extended global encoding kernels for all channels including imaginary message channels and imaginary error channels, which satisfy:

1. $\tilde{f}_{d_i'} = 1_{d_i'}$, $1 \le i \le \omega$, and $\tilde{f}_{e'} = 1_e$, $e \in E'$, where 1_d is an $(\omega + |E|)$-dimensional column vector which is the indicator function of $d \in In(s) \cup E$;
2. for other channel $e \in E$,

$$\tilde{f}_e = \sum_{d \in In(tail(e))} k_{d,e}\tilde{f}_d + 1_e,$$

where $k_{d,e} \in \mathscr{F}$ is the local encoding coefficient for the adjacent pair (d,e) of channels with $d \in In(tail(e))$, and again 1_e is an $(\omega + |E|)$-dimensional column vector which is the indicator function of channel $e \in E$.

In order to illustrate the concepts induced above, we check a simple network, a linear network code and the corresponding linear network error correction code over this network.

Example 3.1. We consider an acyclic network $G = (V,E)$ showed by Fig. 3.1 below. Clearly, $V = \{s,t,i_1,i_2,i_3\}$, where s is the single source node, t is the sink node, and

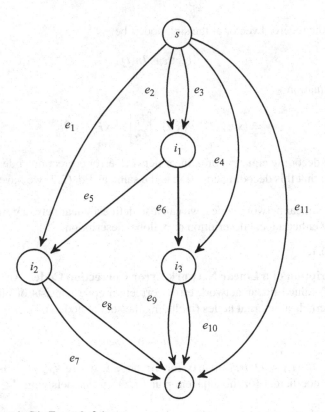

Fig. 3.1 Network G in Example 3.1

i_1, i_2, i_3 are three internal nodes, and $E = \{e_i : 1 \le i \le 11\}$. Let the information rate $\omega = 2$ and the base field be a prime field $\mathbb{F}_{11}$. The linear network code is defined by the local kernels K_s for the source node s, and K_{i_1}, K_{i_2}, K_{i_3} for other three internal nodes i_1, i_2, i_3. They are as follows:

$$K_s = \begin{bmatrix} 1 & 1 & 1 & 1 & 1 \\ 0 & 1 & 2 & 3 & 4 \end{bmatrix}, \quad B = \begin{bmatrix} 1 & 1 & 1 & 1 & 0 & 0 & 0 & 0 & 0 & 0 & 1 \\ 0 & 1 & 2 & 3 & 0 & 0 & 0 & 0 & 0 & 0 & 4 \end{bmatrix},$$

and

$$K_{i_1} = K_{i_2} = K_{i_3} = \begin{bmatrix} 1 & 1 \\ 1 & 2 \end{bmatrix}.$$

Then, the system transfer matrix is as follows:

$$K = \begin{bmatrix} 0 & 0 & 0 & 0 & 0 & 0 & 1 & 1 & 0 & 0 & 0 \\ 0 & 0 & 0 & 0 & 1 & 1 & 0 & 0 & 0 & 0 & 0 \\ 0 & 0 & 0 & 0 & 1 & 2 & 0 & 0 & 0 & 0 & 0 \\ 0 & 0 & 0 & 0 & 0 & 0 & 0 & 0 & 1 & 1 & 0 \\ 0 & 0 & 0 & 0 & 0 & 0 & 1 & 2 & 0 & 0 & 0 \\ 0 & 0 & 0 & 0 & 0 & 0 & 0 & 0 & 1 & 2 & 0 \\ 0 & 0 & 0 & 0 & 0 & 0 & 0 & 0 & 0 & 0 & 0 \\ 0 & 0 & 0 & 0 & 0 & 0 & 0 & 0 & 0 & 0 & 0 \\ 0 & 0 & 0 & 0 & 0 & 0 & 0 & 0 & 0 & 0 & 0 \\ 0 & 0 & 0 & 0 & 0 & 0 & 0 & 0 & 0 & 0 & 0 \\ 0 & 0 & 0 & 0 & 0 & 0 & 0 & 0 & 0 & 0 & 0 \end{bmatrix}.$$

Further, by the simple calculation, we have

$$F = (I - K)^{-1} = I + K + K^2$$

$$= \begin{bmatrix} 1 & 0 & 0 & 0 & 0 & 0 & 1 & 1 & 0 & 0 & 0 \\ 0 & 1 & 0 & 0 & 1 & 1 & 1 & 2 & 1 & 2 & 0 \\ 0 & 0 & 1 & 0 & 1 & 2 & 1 & 2 & 2 & 4 & 0 \\ 0 & 0 & 0 & 1 & 0 & 0 & 0 & 0 & 1 & 1 & 0 \\ 0 & 0 & 0 & 0 & 1 & 0 & 1 & 2 & 0 & 0 & 0 \\ 0 & 0 & 0 & 0 & 0 & 1 & 0 & 0 & 1 & 2 & 0 \\ 0 & 0 & 0 & 0 & 0 & 0 & 1 & 0 & 0 & 0 & 0 \\ 0 & 0 & 0 & 0 & 0 & 0 & 0 & 1 & 0 & 0 & 0 \\ 0 & 0 & 0 & 0 & 0 & 0 & 0 & 0 & 1 & 0 & 0 \\ 0 & 0 & 0 & 0 & 0 & 0 & 0 & 0 & 0 & 1 & 0 \\ 0 & 0 & 0 & 0 & 0 & 0 & 0 & 0 & 0 & 0 & 1 \end{bmatrix}.$$

So the global kernel matrix and the extended global kernel matrix are respective:

$$[f_{e_i} : 1 \leq i \leq 11] = B(I - K)^{-1} = \begin{bmatrix} 1 & 1 & 1 & 1 & 2 & 3 & 3 & 5 & 4 & 7 & 1 \\ 0 & 1 & 2 & 3 & 3 & 5 & 3 & 6 & 8 & 2 & 4 \end{bmatrix},$$

$$[\tilde{f}_{e_i} : 1 \leq i \leq 11] = \begin{bmatrix} B \\ I \end{bmatrix} (I - K)^{-1} = \begin{bmatrix} 1 & 1 & 1 & 1 & 2 & 3 & 3 & 5 & 4 & 7 & 1 \\ 0 & 1 & 2 & 3 & 3 & 5 & 3 & 6 & 8 & 2 & 4 \\ 1 & 0 & 0 & 0 & 0 & 1 & 1 & 0 & 0 & 0 \\ 0 & 1 & 0 & 0 & 1 & 1 & 1 & 2 & 1 & 2 & 0 \\ 0 & 0 & 1 & 0 & 1 & 2 & 1 & 2 & 2 & 4 & 0 \\ 0 & 0 & 0 & 1 & 0 & 0 & 0 & 0 & 1 & 1 & 0 \\ 0 & 0 & 0 & 0 & 1 & 0 & 1 & 2 & 0 & 0 & 0 \\ 0 & 0 & 0 & 0 & 0 & 1 & 0 & 0 & 1 & 2 & 0 \\ 0 & 0 & 0 & 0 & 0 & 0 & 1 & 0 & 0 & 0 & 0 \\ 0 & 0 & 0 & 0 & 0 & 0 & 0 & 1 & 0 & 0 & 0 \\ 0 & 0 & 0 & 0 & 0 & 0 & 0 & 0 & 1 & 0 & 0 \\ 0 & 0 & 0 & 0 & 0 & 0 & 0 & 0 & 0 & 1 & 0 \\ 0 & 0 & 0 & 0 & 0 & 0 & 0 & 0 & 0 & 0 & 1 \end{bmatrix} .$$

Further, for this linear network error correction code, the decoding matrix at the sink node t is:

$$\bar{F}_t = [\tilde{f}_{e_7} \ \tilde{f}_{e_8} \ \tilde{f}_{e_9} \ \tilde{f}_{e_{10}} \ \tilde{f}_{e_{11}}] = \begin{bmatrix} 3 & 5 & 4 & 7 & 1 \\ 3 & 6 & 8 & 2 & 4 \\ 1 & 1 & 0 & 0 & 0 \\ 1 & 2 & 1 & 2 & 0 \\ 1 & 2 & 2 & 4 & 0 \\ 0 & 0 & 1 & 1 & 0 \\ 1 & 2 & 0 & 0 & 0 \\ 0 & 0 & 1 & 2 & 0 \\ 1 & 0 & 0 & 0 & 0 \\ 0 & 1 & 0 & 0 & 0 \\ 0 & 0 & 1 & 0 & 0 \\ 0 & 0 & 0 & 1 & 0 \\ 0 & 0 & 0 & 0 & 1 \end{bmatrix} ,$$

which is obtained from the extended global kernel matrix by taking the columns corresponding the channels in $In(t)$.

At a sink node t, the messages $\{\tilde{U}_e : e \in In(t)\}$ and the extended global encoding kernels $\{\tilde{f}_e : e \in In(t)\}$ are available. For all messages including source messages and error messages, if they are considered as column vectors, then the above discussions describe linear network error correction coding in packet networks [59]. Specifically, in this case, $x_i, z_e,$ and $\tilde{U}_e$ for $1 \leq i \leq \omega, e \in E$ are column vectors on the base field $\mathscr{F}$. All message scalar components in a packet share the same extended global encoding kernel. The minimum distance decoding principle is applied to each message scalar component of the packets.

3.2 Distances and Weights

Recall that an error pattern ρ is regarded as a set of channels in which errors occur, and an error message vector $\mathbf{z}$ matches an error pattern ρ, if $z_e = 0$ for all $e \in E \backslash \rho$. In the following, we define two vector spaces, which are of importance in further discussion.

Definition 3.2. Define

$$\Delta(t,\rho) = \{(\mathbf{0}\ \mathbf{z}) \cdot \tilde{F}_t : \text{ all } \mathbf{z} \in \mathscr{Z} \text{ matching the error pattern } \rho\}$$
$$= \{\mathbf{z}G_t : \text{ all } \mathbf{z} \in \mathscr{Z} \text{ matching the error pattern } \rho\},$$

where $\mathbf{0}$ is an ω-dimensional zero row vector, and

$$\Phi(t) = \{(\mathbf{x}\ \mathbf{0})\tilde{F}_t : \text{ all } \mathbf{x} \in \mathscr{F}^\omega\}$$
$$= \{\mathbf{x}F_t : \text{ all } \mathbf{x} \in \mathscr{F}^\omega\},$$

where $\mathbf{0}$ is an $|E|$-dimensional zero row vector. We say $\Delta(t,\rho)$ and $\Phi(t)$ the error space of the error pattern ρ and the message space with respect to t, respectively.

Let L be a collection of vectors in some linear space. As convenience, we use $\langle L \rangle$ to represent the subspace spanned by the vectors in L. And we use $\text{row}_t(d)$, $d \in In(s) \cup E$, to denote the row vectors of the decoding matrix $\tilde{F}_t$, because all row vectors are indexed by all channels in $In(s) \cup E$. These row vectors are of dimension $|In(t)|$. Actually, we further have

$$\Delta(t,\rho) = \langle\{\text{row}_t(d) : d \in \rho\}\rangle,$$

and

$$\Phi(t) = \langle\{\text{row}_t(d) : d \in In(s)\}\rangle.$$

These row vectors play a important role in linear network error correction coding. And further it is not difficult to see that these vectors have the following relations:

$$\text{row}_t(e) = \sum_{d \in Out(head(e))} k_{e,d} \cdot \text{row}_t(d), \tag{3.3}$$

for any $e \in E$. Moreover, we give other important concepts.

Definition 3.3. We say that an error pattern ρ_1 is dominated by another error pattern ρ_2 with respect to a sink node t if $\Delta(t,\rho_1) \subseteq \Delta(t,\rho_2)$ for any linear network code. This relation is denoted by $\rho_1 \prec_t \rho_2$.

As an example of the introduced definitions, we continue checking the acyclic network G in Example 3.1.

Example 3.2. Consider the same network and linear network code in Example 3.1. For the sink node t and an error pattern $\rho = \{e_3, e_7, e_9\}$, the message space $\Phi(t)$ and the error space $\Delta(t,\rho)$ of the error pattern with respect to t are respective:

$$\Phi(t) = \langle (3\ 5\ 4\ 7\ 1), (3\ 6\ 8\ 2\ 4) \rangle,$$
$$\Delta(t,\rho) = \langle (1\ 2\ 2\ 4\ 0), (1\ 0\ 0\ 0\ 0), (0\ 0\ 1\ 0\ 0) \rangle.$$

Further, it can be easily checked that the error pattern $\{e_1, e_5\}$ is dominated by $\{e_7, e_8\}$. As another example of dominance, let ρ be an error pattern satisfying $\rho \cap In(t) = \emptyset$ and $CUT_{\rho,t}$ be an edge-cut between ρ and t, that is, $CUT_{\rho,t}$ is a set of channels whose removal disconnects ρ from t. Then $CUT_{\rho,t}$ dominates ρ with respect to t.

Definition 3.4. The rank of an error pattern ρ with respect to a sink node t is defined by

$$rank_t(\rho) = \min\{|\rho'| : \rho \prec_t \rho'\},$$

where $|\rho'|$ denotes the cardinality of error pattern ρ'.

The above definition on the rank of an error pattern is abstract, and so in order to understand this concept more intuitively, we give the following proposition.

Proposition 3.1. *For an error pattern ρ, introduce a source node s_ρ. Let $\rho = \{e_1, e_2, \cdots, e_l\}$ where $e_j \in In(i_j)$ for $1 \leq j \leq l$ and define new edges $e'_j = (s_\rho, i_j)$. Replace each e_j by e'_j on the network, that is, add $e'_1, e'_2, \cdots, e'_l$ on the network and delete $e_1, e_2, \cdots, e_l$ from the network. Then the rank of the error pattern ρ with respect to a sink node t in the original network is equal to the minimum cut capacity between s_ρ and t.*

Proof. Let G be the original network. Adding $e'_1, e'_2, \cdots, e'_l$ on G and deleting $e_1, e_2, \cdots, e_l$ from G according to the approach mentioned in the proposition, denote by G' the new network. Let $CUT_{s_\rho,t}$ be an arbitrary cut between s_ρ and t in G'. For any linear network code on G, let $k_{e'_i,d} = k_{e_i,d}$, $1 \leq i \leq l$, for each channel $d \in E$. Then for $1 \leq i \leq l$,

$$\text{row}_t(e'_i) = \text{row}_t(e_i).$$

In addition, it is not difficult to see that any $\text{row}_t(e'_i) = \text{row}_t(e_i)$ is a linear combination of row vectors $\text{row}_t(d)$ for $d \in CUT_{s_\rho,t}$ by applying the formula (3.3) recursively, which implies that

$$\Delta(t,\rho) \subseteq \Delta(t, CUT_{s_\rho,t}).$$

Notice that it is true for any linear network code. So $CUT_{s_\rho,t}$ dominates the error pattern ρ and $rank_t(\rho) \leq |CUT_{s_\rho,t}|$. Furthermore, this conclusion is true for arbitrary cut between s_ρ and t. Therefore, the rank $rank_t(\rho)$ of the error pattern ρ is no more than the minimum cut capacity between s_ρ and t.

On the other hand, for any linear network code,

$$rank_t(\rho) \geq \dim(\Delta(t,\rho)),$$

since

$$rank_t(\rho) = \min\{|\rho'| : \rho \prec_t \rho'\} \geq \min\{\dim(\Delta(t,\rho')) : \rho \prec_t \rho'\} \geq \dim(\Delta(t,\rho)).$$

Let $C_{\rho,t}$ be the minimum cut capacity between s_{ρ} and t on G', and there exist $C_{\rho,t}$ channel-disjoint paths from s_{ρ} to t. Further, assign $k_{d,e} = 1$ for all adjacent pairs of channels d, e if they are in the same path, and $k_{d,e} = 0$ otherwise. For this particular linear network code, it is evident that $\dim(\Delta(t,\rho)) \geq C_{\rho,t}$. This shows $rank_t(\rho) \geq C_{\rho,t}$.

Combining the above, we complete the proof. □

Recall that an error pattern $\rho_{\mathbf{z}}$ induced by the error vector $\mathbf{z}$ is a collection of the channels on which the corresponding coordinates of $\mathbf{z}$ are nonzero. So the rank of an error pattern induced by an error vector $\mathbf{z}$ with respect to a sink node $t \in T$ is defined as:

$$w_r^{(t)}(\mathbf{z}) \triangleq rank_t(\rho_{\mathbf{z}}).$$

In series of papers Zhang et al. [2, 17, 18, 58, 59, 61] etc., they use this concept to measure the seriousness of errors.

Besides the rank of error pattern, the Hamming weight and the dimension of error space to be introduced below are also applied to measure the seriousness of errors.

Definition 3.5.

- *Hamming weight.* The Hamming weight of an error vector $\mathbf{z} = [z_e : e \in E] \in \mathscr{F}^{|E|}$ is defined as the number of its nonzero coordinates, i.e.,

$$w_H(\mathbf{z}) \triangleq |\{z_e \neq 0 : \text{all } e \in E\}|.$$

- *Dimension of error space.* The dimension of the error space $\Lambda(t, \rho_{\mathbf{z}})$ induced by the error vector $\mathbf{z}$ with respect to a sink node $t \in T$ is defined as:

$$w_{\Delta}^{(t)}(\mathbf{z}) = \dim(\Delta(t,\rho_{\mathbf{z}})).$$

Note that for Hamming weight $w_H(\mathbf{z})$, the superscript (t) is not necessary as it is independent of sink nodes in T.

Further, it is evident that all three measures $w_H(\cdot)$, $w_r^{(t)}(\cdot)$ and $w_{\Delta}^{(t)}(\cdot)$ are mappings from $\mathscr{Z}$ to $\mathbb{Z}^+ \cup \{0\}$. But they may not satisfy the second condition of weight measure, that is, there exist distinct error vectors $\mathbf{z}_1, \mathbf{z}_2 \in \mathscr{Z}$ such that $\mathbf{z}_1 G_t = \mathbf{z}_2 G_t$ but $w_H(\mathbf{z}_1) \neq w_H(\mathbf{z}_2)$ (resp. $w_r^{(t)}(\mathbf{z}_1) \neq w_r^{(t)}(\mathbf{z}_2)$ and $w_{\Delta}^{(t)}(\mathbf{z}_1) \neq w_{\Delta}^{(t)}(\mathbf{z}_2)$). Furthermore, it is easy to check the following inequality.

Proposition 3.2. *For any error vector $\mathbf{z} \in \mathscr{Z}$,*

$$w^{(t)}(\mathbf{z}) \leq w_{\Delta}^{(t)}(\mathbf{z}) \leq w_r^{(t)}(\mathbf{z}) \leq w_H(\mathbf{z}). \tag{3.4}$$

Further, we will indicate that any two measures mentioned are not equal by taking an example below, which shows that the above inequality (3.4) is strict, i.e.,

$$w^{(t)}(\mathbf{z}) < w_{\Delta}^{(t)}(\mathbf{z}) < w_r^{(t)}(\mathbf{z}) < w_H(\mathbf{z})$$

for an error vector $\mathbf{z}$ and a linear network error correction code on the network in the following example.

Example 3.3. Consider a simple network below. An one-dimensional $\mathbb{F}_5$-valued linear network error correction code over this network is determined by the local encoding kernels (Fig. 3.2):

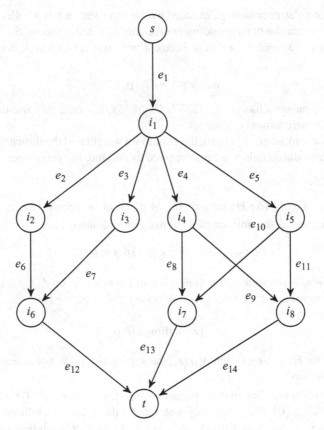

Fig. 3.2 Network G in Example 3.3

$$K_s = \begin{bmatrix} 1 \end{bmatrix}, \ K_{i_1} = \begin{bmatrix} 1 & 1 & 2 & 2 \end{bmatrix}, \ K_{i_2} = K_{i_3} = \begin{bmatrix} 1 \end{bmatrix},$$

$$K_{i_4} = K_{i_5} = \begin{bmatrix} 1 & 1 \end{bmatrix}, \ K_{i_6} = K_{i_7} = K_{i_8} = \begin{bmatrix} 1 \\ 2 \end{bmatrix}.$$

Hence, we deduce $F_t = \begin{bmatrix} 2 & 1 & 1 \end{bmatrix} \neq \mathbf{0}$, and further

$$\text{row}_t(e_1) = (3\ 1\ 1), \ \text{row}_t(e_2) = (1\ 0\ 0), \ \text{row}_t(e_3) = (2\ 0\ 0),$$
$$\text{row}_t(e_4) = (0\ 1\ 1), \ \text{row}_t(e_5) = (0\ 2\ 2).$$

Moreover, let $\mathbf{z} \in \mathscr{F}^{|E|} = \mathbb{F}_5^{14}$ be an error vector with $z_{e_2} = z_{e_3} = 1$, $z_{e_4} = z_{e_5} = 2$, and $z_e = 0$ for others $e \in E \backslash \{e_2, e_3, e_4, e_5\}$. Therefore, after simple calculation, we obtain

- $w_H(\mathbf{z}) = 4$;
- $w_r^{(t)}(\mathbf{z}) = rank_t(\rho_{\mathbf{z}}) = rank_t(\{e_2, e_3, e_4, e_5\}) = 3$;
- $w_\Delta^{(t)}(\mathbf{z}) = \dim(\Delta(r, \rho_{\mathbf{z}})) = \dim(\langle \text{row}_t(e_i) : i = 2, 3, 4, 5 \rangle) = 2$;
- $w^{(t)}(\mathbf{z}) = \min\{w_H(\mathbf{z}') : \mathbf{z}'G_t = \mathbf{z}G_t\}$ and note that

$$\mathbf{z}G_t = \mathbf{z}_{\rho_{\mathbf{z}}} A_{\rho_{\mathbf{z}}} G_t = \begin{pmatrix} 1 & 1 & 2 & 2 \end{pmatrix} \begin{bmatrix} 1 & 0 & 0 \\ 2 & 0 & 0 \\ 0 & 1 & 1 \\ 0 & 2 & 2 \end{bmatrix} = \begin{pmatrix} 3 & 1 & 1 \end{pmatrix} = \text{row}_t(e_1) \triangleq \mathbf{z}'G_t,$$

where $\mathbf{z}' \in \mathbb{F}_5^{14}$ is an error vector with $z_{e_1} = 1$ and $z_e = 0$ for others. Hence, $w^{(t)}(\mathbf{z}) = w_H(\mathbf{z}') = 1$.

Therefore, it follows

$$w^{(t)}(\mathbf{z}) < w_\Delta^{(t)}(\mathbf{z}) < w_r^{(t)}(\mathbf{z}) < w_H(\mathbf{z}).$$

Particularly, for another three measures $w_H(\cdot)$, $w_r^{(t)}(\cdot)$ and $w_\Delta^{(t)}(\cdot)$, we call them *pseudo-weight measures* of error vectors. Further, notice that the pseudo-weight $w_H(\cdot)$ is just determined completely by error vectors, the pseudo-weight $w_r^{(t)}(\cdot)$ is determined completely by error vectors and network topology, and besides error vectors and network topology, the used linear network error correction code which depends on the network topology is required to determine $w_\Delta^{(t)}(\cdot)$. In order to determine $w^{(t)}(\cdot)$, additional calculations are further required besides the above requirements. Therefore, although they are not actual weight, these three pseudo-weights are still very useful and can simply the computing.

Similar to the relationship between Hamming weight and Hamming distance in classical coding theory, $w_H(\cdot)$, $w_r^{(t)}(\cdot)$, $w_\Delta^{(t)}(\cdot)$ and $w^{(t)}(\cdot)$ can also induce the corresponding "distances" as follows. For any two received vectors $\mathbf{y}_1, \mathbf{y}_2 \in \mathscr{Y}_t = \mathscr{F}^{|In(t)|}$, define:

$$d_H^{(t)}(\mathbf{y}_1, \mathbf{y}_2) \triangleq \min\{w_H(\mathbf{z}) : \mathbf{z} \in \mathscr{Z} \text{ such that } \mathbf{y}_1 = \mathbf{y}_2 + \mathbf{z}G_t\};$$

$$d_r^{(t)}(\mathbf{y}_1, \mathbf{y}_2) \triangleq \min\{w_r^{(t)}(\mathbf{z}) : \mathbf{z} \in \mathscr{Z} \text{ such that } \mathbf{y}_1 = \mathbf{y}_2 + \mathbf{z}G_t\}$$
$$= \min\{rank_t(\rho_{\mathbf{z}}) : \mathbf{z} \in \mathscr{Z} \text{ such that } \mathbf{y}_1 = \mathbf{y}_2 + \mathbf{z}G_t\};$$

$$d_\Delta^{(t)}(\mathbf{y}_1, \mathbf{y}_2) \triangleq \min\{w_\Delta^{(t)}(\mathbf{z}) : \mathbf{z} \in \mathscr{Z} \text{ such that } \mathbf{y}_1 = \mathbf{y}_2 + \mathbf{z}G_t\}$$
$$= \min\{\dim(\Delta(t, \rho_{\mathbf{z}})) : \mathbf{z} \in \mathscr{Z} \text{ such that } \mathbf{y}_1 = \mathbf{y}_2 + \mathbf{z}G_t\};$$

$$d_w^{(t)}(\mathbf{y}_1, \mathbf{y}_2) \triangleq \min\{w^{(t)}(\mathbf{z}) : \mathbf{z} \in \mathscr{Z} \text{ such that } \mathbf{y}_1 = \mathbf{y}_2 + \mathbf{z}G_t\}.$$

And note that the distance $d_H^{(t)}(\cdot,\cdot)$ induced by the Hamming weight is the actual distance $d^{(t)}(\cdot,\cdot)$ used above, i.e., $d^{(t)}(\cdot,\cdot) = d_H^{(t)}(\cdot,\cdot)$. For these distance functions, we further have the following result.

Theorem 3.1. *The distance functions* $d_H^{(t)}(\cdot,\cdot)$, $d_r^{(t)}(\cdot,\cdot)$, $d_\Delta^{(t)}(\cdot,\cdot)$, *and* $d_w^{(t)}(\cdot,\cdot)$ *are equivalent, that is, for any two vectors* $\mathbf{y}_1, \mathbf{y}_2 \in \mathscr{Y}_t = \mathscr{F}^{|In(t)|}$,

$$d_H^{(t)}(\mathbf{y}_1,\mathbf{y}_2) = d_r^{(t)}(\mathbf{y}_1,\mathbf{y}_2) = d_\Delta^{(t)}(\mathbf{y}_1,\mathbf{y}_2) = d_w^{(t)}(\mathbf{y}_1,\mathbf{y}_2).$$

Proof. Let $\mathbf{y}_1, \mathbf{y}_2 \in \mathscr{Y}_t$ be arbitrary two received vectors at the sink node $t \in T$. For any error vector $\mathbf{z} \in \mathscr{Z}$ satisfying $\mathbf{y}_1 = \mathbf{y}_2 + \mathbf{z}G_t$, Proposition 3.2 shows

$$w_H(\mathbf{z}) \geq rank_t(\rho_\mathbf{z}) \geq \dim(\Delta(t,\rho_\mathbf{z})) \geq w^{(t)}(\mathbf{z}),$$

i.e.,

$$w_H(\mathbf{z}) \geq w_r^{(t)}(\mathbf{z}) \geq w_\Delta^{(t)}(\mathbf{z}) \geq w^{(t)}(\mathbf{z}),$$

where again $\rho_\mathbf{z}$ is the error pattern induced by the error vector $\mathbf{z}$. This further implies

$$d_H^{(t)}(\mathbf{y}_1,\mathbf{y}_2) \geq d_r^{(t)}(\mathbf{y}_1,\mathbf{y}_2) \geq d_\Delta^{(t)}(\mathbf{y}_1,\mathbf{y}_2) \geq d_w^{(t)}(\mathbf{y}_1,\mathbf{y}_2).$$

So it suffices to prove $d_H^{(t)}(\mathbf{y}_1,\mathbf{y}_2) \leq d_w^{(t)}(\mathbf{y}_1,\mathbf{y}_2)$.
We know that

$$d_w^{(t)}(\mathbf{y}_1,\mathbf{y}_2) = \min\{w^{(t)}(\mathbf{z}) : \mathbf{z} \in \mathscr{Z} \text{ such that } \mathbf{y}_1 = \mathbf{y}_2 + \mathbf{z}G_t\}.$$

Hence, without loss of generality, we further assume that $\mathbf{z} \in \mathscr{Z}$ is an error vector satisfying $\mathbf{y}_1 = \mathbf{y}_2 + \mathbf{z}G_t$ and $w^{(t)}(\mathbf{z}) = d_w^{(t)}(\mathbf{y}_1,\mathbf{y}_2)$. Together with

$$w^{(t)}(\mathbf{z}) = \min\{w_H(\mathbf{z}') : \mathbf{z}' \in \mathscr{Z} \text{ such that } \mathbf{z}'G_t = \mathbf{z}G_t\},$$

there exist an error vector $\mathbf{z}' \in \mathscr{Z}$ satisfying $w_H(\mathbf{z}') = w^{(t)}(\mathbf{z})$ and $\mathbf{z}'G_t = \mathbf{z}G_t$, which leads to

$$w_H(\mathbf{z}') = w^{(t)}(\mathbf{z}) = d_w^{(t)}(\mathbf{y}_1,\mathbf{y}_2).$$

On the other hand, one has

$$d_H^{(t)}(\mathbf{y}_1,\mathbf{y}_2) = \min\{w_H(\hat{\mathbf{z}}) : \hat{\mathbf{z}} \in \mathscr{Z} \text{ such that } \mathbf{y}_1 = \mathbf{y}_2 + \hat{\mathbf{z}}G_t\} \leq w_H(\mathbf{z}') = d_w^{(t)}(\mathbf{y}_1,\mathbf{y}_2)$$

by $\mathbf{y}_1 = \mathbf{y}_2 + \mathbf{z}'G_t$. This completes the proof.   □

Combining the above Theorems 3.1 and 2.1, we obtain the following corollary.

Corollary 3.1. *All four equivalent distance functions* $d_H^{(t)}(\cdot,\cdot)$, $d_r^{(t)}(\cdot,\cdot)$, $d_\Delta^{(t)}(\cdot,\cdot)$ *and* $d_w^{(t)}(\cdot,\cdot)$ *satisfy the following properties: for any* $\mathbf{y}_1, \mathbf{y}_2, \mathbf{y}_3 \in \mathscr{Y}_t$,

1. $d^{(t)}(\mathbf{y}_1,\mathbf{y}_2) \geq 0$, *and* $d^{(t)}(\mathbf{y}_1,\mathbf{y}_2) = 0$ *if and only if* $\mathbf{y}_1 = \mathbf{y}_2$;
2. $d^{(t)}(\mathbf{y}_1,\mathbf{y}_2) = d^{(t)}(\mathbf{y}_2,\mathbf{y}_1)$;
3. $d^{(t)}(\mathbf{y}_1,\mathbf{y}_3) \leq d^{(t)}(\mathbf{y}_1,\mathbf{y}_2) + d^{(t)}(\mathbf{y}_2,\mathbf{y}_3)$;

where $d^{(t)}(\cdot,\cdot)$ represents any one of the four distance functions $d_H^{(t)}(\cdot,\cdot)$, $d_r^{(t)}(\cdot,\cdot)$, $d_\Delta^{(t)}(\cdot,\cdot)$ and $d_w^{(t)}(\cdot,\cdot)$.

Subsequently, we have the following result.

Corollary 3.2. *For any error vector $\mathbf{z} \in \mathscr{Z}$, the weight of $\mathbf{z}$ has the following equivalent forms:*

$$
\begin{aligned}
w^{(t)}(\mathbf{z}) = d_H^{(t)}(\mathbf{0}, \mathbf{z}G_t) &= \min\{w_H(\mathbf{z}') : \; all \; \mathbf{z}' \in \mathscr{Z} \; such \; that \; \mathbf{z}'G_t = \mathbf{z}G_t\} \\
&= d_r^{(t)}(\mathbf{0}, \mathbf{z}G_t) = \min\{rank_t(\rho_{\mathbf{z}'}) : \; all \; \mathbf{z}' \in \mathscr{Z} \; such \; that \; \mathbf{z}'G_t = \mathbf{z}G_t\} \\
&= d_\Delta^{(t)}(\mathbf{0}, \mathbf{z}G_t) = \min\{\dim(\Delta(t, \rho_{\mathbf{z}'})) : \; all \; \mathbf{z}' \in \mathscr{Z} \; such \; that \; \mathbf{z}'G_t = \mathbf{z}G_t\} \\
&= d_w^{(t)}(\mathbf{0}, \mathbf{z}G_t) = \min\{w^{(t)}(\mathbf{z}') : \; all \; \mathbf{z}' \in \mathscr{Z} \; such \; that \; \mathbf{z}'G_t = \mathbf{z}G_t\}.
\end{aligned}
$$

We have known that the minimum distance of linear network error correction codes at the sink node $t \in T$ is as follows:

$$
d_{\min}^{(t)} = \min\{d^{(t)}(\mathbf{x}_1 F_t, \mathbf{x}_2 F_t) : \; all \; \mathbf{x}_1, \mathbf{x}_2 \in \mathscr{X} \; with \; \mathbf{x}_1 \neq \mathbf{x}_2\}.
$$

On the other hand, in Zhang [59] and Guang et al. [18] etc., they define another minimum distance of linear network error correction codes at the sink node $t \in T$ by applying message space and error space as:

$$
d_{\min}^{(t)} = \min\{rank_t(\rho) : \; \Phi(t) \cap \Delta(t, \rho) \neq \{\mathbf{0}\}\}.
$$

As mentioned above, we always consider regular linear network error correction codes, that is, $\dim(\Phi(t)) = \omega$ for any sink node $t \in T$ in this case.

Example 3.4. Continue discussing the network and the linear network error correction code in Example 3.1, by checking the row vectors of the decoding matrix $\tilde{F}_t$, we can see that the intersections of all three dimensional error spaces with the message space are $\{\mathbf{0}\}$. This implies that the minimum distance of this code at t is 4.

Similarly, this minimum distance also plays the same role as it does in classical coding theory, which characterizes the error correction/detection capabilities of a linear network error correction code. In the following, we give a proposition on this minimum distance.

Proposition 3.3. *For the minimum distance of a regular linear network error correction code at a sink node t, there exist the following equalities:*

$$
\begin{aligned}
d_{\min}^{(t)} &= \min\{rank_t(\rho) : \; \Phi(t) \cap \Delta(t, \rho) \neq \{\mathbf{0}\}\} & (3.5) \\
&= \min\{|\rho| : \; \Phi(t) \cap \Delta(t, \rho) \neq \{\mathbf{0}\}\} & (3.6) \\
&= \min\{\dim(\Delta(t, \rho)) : \; \Phi(t) \cap \Delta(t, \rho) \neq \{\mathbf{0}\}\}. & (3.7)
\end{aligned}
$$

Proof. We define the set of error patterns

$$\Pi \triangleq \{\rho \subseteq E : \Phi(t) \cap \Delta(t,\rho) \neq \{\mathbf{0}\}\}.$$

Then one has

$$(3.5) = \min_{\rho \in \Pi} rank_t(\rho), \ (3.6) = \min_{\rho \in \Pi} |\rho|, \ (3.7) = \min_{\rho \in \Pi} \dim(\Delta(t,\rho)).$$

Since $\dim(\Delta(t,\rho)) \leq rank_t(\rho) \leq |\rho|$ for any error pattern $\rho \subseteq E$, it follows that

$$\min_{\rho \in \Pi} \dim(\Delta(t,\rho)) \leq \min_{\rho \in \Pi} rank_t(\rho) \leq \min_{\rho \in \Pi} |\rho|.$$

It is enough to prove $\min_{\rho \in \Pi} |\rho| \leq \min_{\rho \in \Pi} \dim(\Delta(t,\rho))$, in view of the inequalities above. Let $\rho' \in \Pi$ be an error pattern satisfying

$$\dim(\Delta(t,\rho')) = \min_{\rho \in \Pi} \dim(\Delta(t,\rho)).$$

Assume that $\rho' = \{e_1, e_2, \cdots, e_l\}$, which means

$$\Delta(t,\rho') = \langle \{row_t(e_i) : 1 \leq i \leq l\} \rangle.$$

For $\{row_t(e_i) : 1 \leq i \leq l\}$, let its maximum independent vector set be $\{row_t(e_{i_j}) : 1 \leq j \leq m\}$, where $m = \dim(\Delta(t,\rho')) \leq l$. Set $\rho_1 = \{e_{i_j} : 1 \leq j \leq m\}$. This implies that

$$|\rho_1| = \dim(\Delta(t,\rho_1)) = \dim(\Delta(t,\rho'))$$

and

$$\Delta(t,\rho_1) \cap \Phi(t) = \Delta(t,\rho') \cap \Phi(t) \neq \{\mathbf{0}\}.$$

Therefore,

$$\min_{\rho \in \Pi} |\rho| \leq |\rho_1| = \dim(\Delta(t,\rho')) = \min_{\rho \in \Pi} \dim(\Delta(t,\rho)).$$

The proof is completed.   □

In order to distinguish these two minimum distances, we use $d_{\min,1}^{(t)}$ to denote the first one, and use $d_{\min,2}^{(t)}$ to denote the other one. To be specific,

$$d_{\min,1}^{(t)} = \min\{d^{(t)}(\mathbf{x}_1 F_t, \mathbf{x}_2 F_t) : \text{all } \mathbf{x}_1, \mathbf{x}_2 \in \mathscr{X} \text{ with } \mathbf{x}_1 \neq \mathbf{x}_2\};$$

$$d_{\min,2}^{(t)} = \min\{rank_t(\rho) : \Phi(t) \cap \Delta(t,\rho) \neq \{\mathbf{0}\}\}.$$

In the following, we will show that these two minimum distances are no difference.

Theorem 3.2. *For any linear network error correction code on networks,*

$$d_{\min,1}^{(t)} = d_{\min,2}^{(t)}.$$

Proof. First, denote $d_{\min,i}^{(t)}$ by d_i, $i = 1,2$, for simplicity. From Proposition 3.3 and the definition

$$d_2 = \min\{\dim(\Delta(t,\rho)): \ \Phi(t) \cap \Delta(t,\rho) \neq \{\mathbf{0}\}\},$$

there exists an error pattern ρ with $|\rho| = \dim(\Delta(t,\rho)) = d_2$ satisfying

$$\Phi(t) \cap \Delta(t,\rho) \neq \{\mathbf{0}\}.$$

That is, there exists a nonzero message vector $\mathbf{x} \in \mathscr{X}$ and an error vector $\mathbf{z} \in \mathscr{Z}$ matching the error pattern ρ such that $\mathbf{0} \neq \mathbf{x}F_t = \mathbf{z}G_t$. Thus, for any message vector $\mathbf{x}' \in \mathscr{X}$ (or equivalently, the codeword $\mathbf{x}'F_t \in \mathscr{C}_t$), we have

$$\mathbf{x}'F_t + \mathbf{x}F_t = \mathbf{x}'F_t + \mathbf{z}G_t,$$

which implies that

$$d_1 \leq d^{(t)}((\mathbf{x}' + \mathbf{x})F_t, \mathbf{x}'F_t) \tag{3.8}$$

$$= \min\{\dim(\Delta(t,\rho_{\mathbf{z}'})): \ \mathbf{z}' \in \mathscr{Z} \text{ such that } \mathbf{x}'F_t + \mathbf{x}F_t = \mathbf{x}'F_t + \mathbf{z}'G_t\} \tag{3.9}$$

$$\leq \dim(\Delta(t,\rho_{\mathbf{z}})) = \dim(\Delta(t,\rho)) = d_2, \tag{3.10}$$

where inequality (3.8) follows because both $(\mathbf{x}' + \mathbf{x})F_t$ and $\mathbf{x}'F_t$ are codewords at the sink node t, the equality (3.9) follows from Theorem 3.1, and the first equality in (3.10) follows from $\rho_{\mathbf{z}} = \rho$.

On the other hand, let $\mathbf{x}_1$ and $\mathbf{x}_2$ be two distinct message vectors in $\mathscr{X}$ such that $d^{(t)}(\mathbf{x}_1 F_t, \mathbf{x}_2 F_t) = d_1$. Together with

$$d^{(t)}(\mathbf{x}_1 F_t, \mathbf{x}_2 F_t) = \min\{\dim(\Delta(t,\rho_{\mathbf{z}})): \ \mathbf{z} \in \mathscr{Z} \text{ such that } \mathbf{x}_1 F_t = \mathbf{x}_2 F_t + \mathbf{z}G_t\},$$

it is shown that there exists an error vector $\mathbf{z} \in \mathscr{Z}$ such that

$$\mathbf{x}_1 F_t = \mathbf{x}_2 F_t + \mathbf{z}G_t, \text{ and } \dim(\Delta(t,\rho_{\mathbf{z}})) = d_1.$$

We further have

$$(\mathbf{x}_1 - \mathbf{x}_2)F_t = \mathbf{z}G_t, \text{ and } (\mathbf{x}_1 - \mathbf{x}_2)F_t \neq \mathbf{0}$$

as $\mathbf{x}_1$ and $\mathbf{x}_2$ are distinct and the matrix F_t is full-rank. Subsequently, notice that $\mathbf{0} \neq (\mathbf{x}_1 - \mathbf{x}_2)F_t \in \Phi(t)$ and $\mathbf{0} \neq \mathbf{z}G_t \in \Delta(t,\rho_{\mathbf{z}})$, which leads to $\Phi(t) \cap \Delta(t,\rho_{\mathbf{z}}) \neq \{\mathbf{0}\}$. Thus, it follows that

$$d_2 = \min\{\dim(\Delta(t,\rho)): \ \Phi(t) \cap \Delta(t,\rho) \neq \{\mathbf{0}\}\} \leq \dim(\Delta(t,\rho_{\mathbf{z}})) = d_1.$$

Combining two directions, we obtain $d_1 = d_2$, which proves the theorem. $\qquad\square$

3.3 Decoding

Recall Minimum Distance Decoding Principle at the sink node $t \in T$. Let $\mathbf{y}_t \in \mathcal{Y}_t$ be a received vector at the sink node $t \in T$, then Minimum Distance Decoding Principle is:

$$D_d^{(t)}(\mathbf{y}_t) \triangleq \arg\min_{\mathbf{x} \in \mathcal{X}} d^{(t)}(\mathbf{x}F_t, \mathbf{y}_t). \tag{3.11}$$

Subsequently, the above Eq. (3.11) can be written as:

$$D_d^{(t)}(\mathbf{y}_t) = \arg\min_{\mathbf{x} \in \mathcal{X}} d^{(t)}(\mathbf{x}F_t, \mathbf{y}_t)$$

$$= \arg\min_{\mathbf{x} \in \mathcal{X}} W^{(t)}(\mathbf{x}F_t - \mathbf{y}_t). \tag{3.12}$$

Since the matrix G_t is full-rank, i.e., $\text{Rank}(G_t) = |In(t)|$, for any $\mathbf{x} \in \mathcal{X}$, there must exist an error vector $\mathbf{z} \in \mathcal{Z}$ such that

$$\mathbf{z}G_t = \mathbf{x}F_t - \mathbf{y}_t, \tag{3.13}$$

and we use $\mathbf{z}(\mathbf{x}, \mathbf{y}_t)$ to denote any one of such error vectors satisfying Eq. (3.13). Notice that all such error vectors have the same weight from Proposition 2.2. So together with the above, we further obtain

$$D_d^{(t)}(\mathbf{y}_t) = \arg\min_{\mathbf{x} \in \mathcal{X}} W^{(t)}(\mathbf{x}F_t - \mathbf{y}_t)$$

$$= \arg\min_{\mathbf{x} \in \mathcal{X}} W^{(t)}(\mathbf{z}(\mathbf{x}, \mathbf{y}_t) \cdot G_t)$$

$$= \arg\min_{\mathbf{x} \in \mathcal{X}} w^{(t)}(\mathbf{z}(\mathbf{x}, \mathbf{y}_t)). \tag{3.14}$$

Further, recall from Corollary 3.2

$$w^{(t)}(\mathbf{z}) = \min\{w_H(\mathbf{z}') : \text{all } \mathbf{z}' \in \mathcal{Z} \text{ such that } \mathbf{z}'G_t = \mathbf{z}G_t\}$$

$$= \min\{w_r^{(t)}(\mathbf{z}') = rank_t(\mathbf{z}') : \text{all } \mathbf{z}' \in \mathcal{Z} \text{ such that } \mathbf{z}'G_t = \mathbf{z}G_t\}$$

$$= \min\{w_\Delta^{(t)}(\mathbf{z}') = \dim(\Delta(t, \rho_{\mathbf{z}'})) : \text{all } \mathbf{z}' \in \mathcal{Z} \text{ such that } \mathbf{z}'G_t = \mathbf{z}G_t\}.$$

Denote by $\mathbf{z}_H(\mathbf{x}, \mathbf{y}_t)$ one of error vectors in $\mathcal{Z}$ satisfying:

$$\mathbf{z}_H(\mathbf{x}, \mathbf{y}_t) \cdot G_t = \mathbf{z}(\mathbf{x}, \mathbf{y}_t) \cdot G_t,$$

and

$$w_H(\mathbf{z}_H(\mathbf{x}, \mathbf{y}_t)) = w^{(t)}(\mathbf{z}(\mathbf{x}, \mathbf{y}_t)).$$

Notice that the Hamming weight of $\mathbf{z}_H(\mathbf{x}, \mathbf{y}_t)$ is the minimum amongst all error vectors $\mathbf{z} \in \mathcal{Z}$ satisfying $\mathbf{z} \cdot G_t = \mathbf{z}(\mathbf{x}, \mathbf{y}_t) \cdot G_t$.

Similarly, denote by $\mathbf{z}_r^{(t)}(\mathbf{x}, \mathbf{y}_t)$ (resp. $\mathbf{z}_\Delta^{(t)}(\mathbf{x}, \mathbf{y}_t)$) one of error vectors in $\mathscr{Z}$ satisfying:

$$\mathbf{z}_r^{(t)}(\mathbf{x}, \mathbf{y}_t) \cdot G_t = \mathbf{z}(\mathbf{x}, \mathbf{y}_t) \cdot G_t,$$

$$(\text{resp. } \mathbf{z}_\Delta^{(t)}(\mathbf{x}, \mathbf{y}_t) \cdot G_t = \mathbf{z}(\mathbf{x}, \mathbf{y}_t) \cdot G_t,)$$

and

$$w_r^{(t)}(\mathbf{z}_r^{(t)}(\mathbf{x}, \mathbf{y}_t)) = w^{(t)}(\mathbf{z}(\mathbf{x}, \mathbf{y}_t)).$$

$$(\text{resp. } w_\Delta^{(t)}(\mathbf{z}_\Delta^{(t)}(\mathbf{x}, \mathbf{y}_t)) = w^{(t)}(\mathbf{z}(\mathbf{x}, \mathbf{y}_t)).)$$

Notice that the rank (resp. the dimension) of the error pattern induced by the error vector $\mathbf{z}_r^{(t)}(\mathbf{x}, \mathbf{y}_t)$ (resp. $\mathbf{z}_\Delta^{(t)}(\mathbf{x}, \mathbf{y}_t)$) achieves the minimum amongst all error vectors $\mathbf{z} \in \mathscr{Z}$ satisfying $\mathbf{z} \cdot G_t = \mathbf{z}(\mathbf{x}, \mathbf{y}_t) \cdot G_t$.

Thus, Eq. (3.14) can further be written as

$$D_d^{(t)}(\mathbf{y}_t) = \arg \min_{\mathbf{x} \in \mathscr{X}} w^{(t)}(\mathbf{z}(\mathbf{x}, \mathbf{y}_t))$$

$$= \arg \min_{\mathbf{x} \in \mathscr{X}} w_H(\mathbf{z}_H(\mathbf{x}, \mathbf{y}_t)) \tag{3.15}$$

$$= \arg \min_{\mathbf{x} \in \mathscr{X}} w_r^{(t)}(\mathbf{z}_r^{(t)}(\mathbf{x}, \mathbf{y}_t)) \tag{3.16}$$

$$= \arg \min_{\mathbf{x} \in \mathscr{X}} w_\Delta^{(t)}(\mathbf{z}_\Delta^{(t)}(\mathbf{x}, \mathbf{y}_t)). \tag{3.17}$$

In addition, (3.14)–(3.17) are called *minimum weight decoding (or minimum network Hamming weight decoding), minimum Hamming weight decoding, minimum rank decoding*, and *minimum dimension decoding* at the sink node $t \in T$, and denoted by $D^{(t)}(\cdot)$, $D_H^{(t)}(\cdot)$, $D_r^{(t)}(\cdot)$, and $D_\Delta^{(t)}(\cdot)$, respectively.

Therefore, a brute force algorithm can be proposed for decoding linear network error correction codes.

A Brute Force Decoding Algorithm:

- Check all error patterns ρ in a non-decreasing order of cardinality up to $\frac{1}{2}(d_{\min}^{(t)} - 1)$. Solve the equation:

$$(\mathbf{x} \ \mathbf{z}_\rho) \tilde{F}_t^\rho = \mathbf{y}_t,$$

where $\tilde{F}_t^\rho \triangleq \begin{bmatrix} F_t \\ A_\rho G_t \end{bmatrix}$. Hence, the above equation can be written as:

$$(\mathbf{x} \ \mathbf{z}_\rho) \begin{bmatrix} F_t \\ A_\rho G_t \end{bmatrix} = \mathbf{y}_t, \tag{3.18}$$

or equivalently,

$$\mathbf{x} F_t + \mathbf{z}_\rho A_\rho G_t = \mathbf{y}_t.$$

If Eq. (3.18) has solutions, then we claim that the error pattern ρ is solvable and record the message parts **x** of the solutions.

- The rank of the first solvable error pattern found in this order is the minimum rank. Let this minimum rank be r.
- If $r \leq \frac{1}{2}(d_{\min}^{(t)} - 1)$, claim that the message part **x** of the first solution found is the decoded source message.
- If up to error pattern cardinality $\frac{1}{2}(d_{\min}^{(t)} - 1)$, no solvable error pattern is found, then claim that the error is not correctable.

For general solvable error patterns ρ, the solutions of Eq. (3.18) may be not unique, but it must be unique for solvable error patterns satisfying $rank_t(\rho) \leq \frac{1}{2}(d_{\min}^{(t)} - 1)$. Further, we say the solutions corresponding to the error patterns of the minimum rank as the minimum rank solutions. The solution we are seeking for should be minimum rank solutions. If there exist two minimum rank solutions leading to different message parts, then the error should be considered uncorrectable. The above brute force method to find the minimum rank solutions is of very high complexity. To lower the decoding complexity, one possible idea is to identify the error pattern for the true error message, called *active error pattern*, by some methods. If the active error pattern is identified, then the rest of the decoding is just solving the decoding equation by using this error pattern. Its complexity is linear in packet length. In [58] and [59], a statistical method for identifying such an active error pattern was proposed, which leads to a so-called statistical decoding of LNEC codes, applicable for packet codes. The performance of this algorithm was analyzed in an unpublished work by Yan et al. [48] and briefly discussed in [62] and [60].

Chapter 4
Coding Bounds of Linear Network Error Correction Codes

As far as we know, there are many different types of coding bounds in classical coding theory, which can measure the efficiency of a code. Similarly, some important and useful coding bounds in classical coding theory are generalized to network error correction coding. This problem was first studied by Cai and Yeung in series of papers [4, 5, 54], which proposed Hamming bound, Gilbert-Varshamov bound and Singleton bound. While the former two bounds are both interesting theoretical results, the Singleton bound plays a very important role in the theory of network error correction. In this chapter, we will discuss these different bounds for linear network error correction codes.

4.1 Hamming Bound

First, we discuss the Hamming Bound of linear network error correction codes as a generalization of the corresponding Hamming bound in classical coding theory.

Theorem 4.1 (Hamming Bound). *Consider a linear network error correction code over a network. Then the number $|\mathscr{C}_t|$ of codewords at the sink node $t \in T$ satisfies:*

$$|\mathscr{C}_t| = q^\omega \leq \frac{q^{|In(t)|}}{\sum_{i=0}^{\tau^{(t)}} \binom{|In(t)|}{i}(q-1)^i},$$

where ω is the information rate, $\tau^{(t)} = \lfloor (d_{\min}^{(t)} - 1)/2 \rfloor$ with $\lfloor \cdot \rfloor$ denoting the floor function and $d_{\min}^{(t)}$ being the minimum distance of the linear network error correction code at the sink node t, and q is the size of base field, i.e., $|\mathscr{F}| = q$.

Proof. The proof of this theorem is similar to that of the Hamming bound in classical coding theory. First, for each codeword $\mathbf{x}F_t \in \mathscr{C}_t$, define a packing sphere $S(\mathbf{x}F_t, \tau^{(t)})$ as:

X. Guang and Z. Zhang, *Linear Network Error Correction Coding*, SpringerBriefs in Computer Science, DOI 10.1007/978-1-4939-0588-1_4, © The Author(s) 2014

$$S(\mathbf{x}F_t, \tau^{(t)}) \triangleq \{\mathbf{y}: \text{all } \mathbf{y} \in \mathscr{F}^{|In(t)|} \text{ such that } d^{(t)}(\mathbf{x}F_t, \mathbf{y}) \leq \tau^{(t)}\}.$$

Further, for any two distinct message vectors $\mathbf{x}_1, \mathbf{x}_2 \in \mathscr{F}^\omega$ (or equivalently, any two distinct codewords $\mathbf{x}_1 F_t, \mathbf{x}_2 F_t$ in $\mathscr{C}_t$), the packing spheres $S(\mathbf{x}_1 F_t, \tau^{(t)})$ and $S(\mathbf{x}_2 F_t, \tau^{(t)})$ are disjoint, i.e.,

$$S(\mathbf{x}_1 F_t, \tau^{(t)}) \cap S(\mathbf{x}_1 F_t, \tau^{(t)}) = \emptyset,$$

since the minimum distance at the sink node t satisfies $\tau^{(t)} = \lfloor (d_{\min}^{(t)} - 1)/2 \rfloor$. Furthermore, we have

$$\bigcup_{\mathbf{x} \in \mathscr{F}^\omega} S(\mathbf{x}F_t, \tau^{(t)}) \subseteq \mathscr{F}^{|In(t)|},$$

where note that the union on the left hand side is a disjoint union. Subsequently, we have

$$\sum_{\mathbf{x} \in \mathscr{F}^\omega} |S(\mathbf{x}F_t, \tau^{(t)})| \leq q^{|In(t)|}.$$

And it is not difficult to see that for any codewords $\mathbf{x}_1 F_t, \mathbf{x}_2 F_t \in \mathscr{C}_t$, the sizes of two corresponding packing spheres are equal, i.e.,

$$|S(\mathbf{x}_1 F_t, \tau^{(t)})| = |S(\mathbf{x}_2 F_t, \tau^{(t)})|.$$

In addition, note that for any two vectors $\mathbf{y}_1, \mathbf{y}_2 \in \mathscr{F}^{|In(t)|}$,

$$
\begin{aligned}
d^{(t)}(\mathbf{y}_1, \mathbf{y}_2) &= W^{(t)}(\mathbf{y}_1 - \mathbf{y}_2) \\
&= \min\{w_H(\mathbf{z}): \mathbf{z} \in \mathscr{Z} \text{ such that } \mathbf{y}_1 - \mathbf{y}_2 = \mathbf{z}G_t\} \\
&\leq w_H(\mathbf{y}_1 - \mathbf{y}_2).
\end{aligned}
$$

Thus, one has

$$
\begin{aligned}
S_H(\mathbf{x}F_t, \tau^{(t)}) &\triangleq \{\mathbf{y}: \text{all } \mathbf{y} \in \mathscr{F}^{|In(t)|} \text{ such that } w_H(\mathbf{x}F_t - \mathbf{y}) \leq \tau^{(t)}\} \\
&\subseteq S(\mathbf{x}F_t, \tau^{(t)}),
\end{aligned}
$$

which leads to

$$|S_H(\mathbf{x}F_t, \tau^{(t)})| \leq |S(\mathbf{x}F_t, \tau^{(t)})|.$$

Together with

$$|S_H(\mathbf{x}F_t, \tau^{(t)})| = \sum_{i=0}^{\tau^{(t)}} \binom{|In(t)|}{i} (q-1)^i,$$

we deduce

$$q^\omega = |\mathscr{C}_t| \leq \frac{q^{|In(t)|}}{|S(\mathbf{x}F_t, \tau^{(t)})|} \leq \frac{q^{|In(t)|}}{|S_H(\mathbf{x}F_t, \tau^{(t)})|} \leq \frac{q^{|In(t)|}}{\sum_{i=0}^{\tau^{(t)}} \binom{|In(t)|}{i} (q-1)^i},$$

where $\mathbf{x}F_t$ is an arbitrary codeword in $\mathscr{C}_t$, which completes the proof. $\qquad \square$

Actually, we can obtain a more general result as follows.

Theorem 4.2. *Consider a linear network error correction code over a network. For any sink node $t \in T$, let CUT_t denote an arbitrary cut between the source node s and the sink node t. Then the number $|\mathscr{C}_t|$ of codewords at the sink node t satisfies:*

$$|\mathscr{C}_t| = q^\omega \le \frac{q^{r_t}}{\sum_{i=0}^{\tau^{(t)}} \binom{r_t}{i}(q-1)^i}, \tag{4.1}$$

where q is the size of the base field $\mathscr{F}$, $\tau^{(t)} = \lfloor (d_{\min}^{(t)} - 1)/2 \rfloor$ with $d_{\min}^{(t)}$ being the minimum distance at the sink node $t \in T$, and r_t is the rank of the matrix $A_{CUT_t} G_t$, or equivalently, the dimension of the error space $\Delta(t, CUT_t)$.

Proof. For the sink node $t \in T$, recall that $\tilde{F}_t = [\tilde{f}_e : e \in In(t)]$ is the decoding matrix at t, and the row vectors of $\tilde{F}_t$ can be indexed by all channels in $In(s) \cup E$, that is,

$$\tilde{F}_t = \begin{bmatrix} \text{row}_t(d_i') : 1 \le i \le \omega \\ \text{row}_t(e) : \quad e \in E \end{bmatrix} = \begin{bmatrix} F_t \\ G_t \end{bmatrix}.$$

Note that the code is regular, i.e., $\text{Rank}(F_t) = \omega$, which shows that the encoding function $\text{En}^{(t)}$ is injective, where recall that

$$\text{En}^{(t)} : \mathscr{F}^\omega \to \mathscr{F}^{|In(t)|}$$

$$\mathbf{x} \mapsto \mathbf{x} \cdot F_t.$$

For the cut CUT_t, consider an $\omega \times |CUT_t|$ matrix $F_{CUT_t} = [f_e : e \in CUT_t]$ with all column vectors f_e, $e \in CUT_t$. Then we claim $\text{Rank}(F_{CUT_t}) = \omega$. Conversely, assume the contrary that $\text{Rank}(F_{CUT_t}) < \omega$. Notice that $\{f_e : e \in In(t)\}$ are linear combinations of $\{f_e : e \in CUT_t\}$ from the following important relation between global encoding kernels in linear network coding theory:

$$f_e = \sum_{d \in In(tail(e))} k_{d,e} f_d,$$

which shows

$$\text{Rank}(F_t) = \text{Rank}([f_e : e \in In(t)]) \le \text{Rank}([f_e : e \in CUT_t]) = \text{Rank}(F_{CUT_t}) < \omega.$$

This is a contradiction. Thus, we can similarly define an injective encoding mapping $\text{En}^{(CUT_t)}$ for the cut CUT_t, that is,

$$\text{En}^{(CUT_t)} : \mathscr{F}^\omega \to \mathscr{F}^{|CUT_t|}$$

$$\mathbf{x} \mapsto \mathbf{x} \cdot F_{CUT_t}.$$

Actually, if there are no errors happened when the message $\mathbf{x}$ is transmitted by this code over the network, the sink node t and the cut CUT_t receive the vectors $\mathbf{x}F_t$ and $\mathbf{x}F_{CUT_t}$, respectively. Furthermore, for any source message vector $\mathbf{x} \in \mathscr{F}^\omega$, it follows that

$$\mathbf{x} \cdot F_{CUT_t} \cdot A_{CUT_t} \cdot (I - K)^{-1} \cdot A_{In(t)}^\top = \mathbf{x} \cdot F_t. \tag{4.2}$$

Thus, let $\mathscr{C}_{CUT_t} = \{\mathbf{x} F_{CUT_t} : \text{all } \mathbf{x} \in \mathscr{F}^\omega\}$ and it follows $|\mathscr{C}_{CUT_t}| = |\mathscr{C}_t| = q^\omega$.

In addition, by the Koetter-Médard Formula (3.1) for linear network error correction codes

$$[\tilde{f}_e : e \in E] = \begin{bmatrix} B \\ I \end{bmatrix} (I - K)^{-1} = \begin{bmatrix} B(I-K)^{-1} \\ (I-K)^{-1} \end{bmatrix},$$

together with

$$\tilde{F}_t = [\tilde{f}_e : e \in In(t)] = \begin{bmatrix} F_t \\ G_t \end{bmatrix},$$

we obtain

$$A_{CUT_t} \cdot (I - K)^{-1} \cdot A_{In(t)}^\top = A_{CUT_t} \cdot G_t = [\text{row}_t(e) : e \in CUT_t] \triangleq G_t^{CUT_t}.$$

Hence, Eq. (4.2) can be rewritten as

$$\mathbf{x} \cdot F_{CUT_t} \cdot A_{CUT_t} \cdot (I - K)^{-1} \cdot A_{In(t)}^\top = \mathbf{x} \cdot F_{CUT_t} \cdot G_t^{CUT_t} = \mathbf{x} \cdot F_t. \tag{4.3}$$

Since $\text{Rank}(G_t^{CUT_t}) = \dim(\Delta(t, CUT_t)) = r_t$, there exists an error pattern $\rho \subseteq CUT_t$ satisfying $|\rho| = r_t$ and $G_t^\rho \triangleq A_\rho G_t$ full-rank, that is,

$$\text{Rank}(G_t^\rho) = \dim(\Delta(t, \rho)) = r_t,$$

which further means that $\{\text{row}_t(e) : e \in \rho\}$ are linearly independent. Thus, for any $\mathbf{y} \in \mathscr{C}_{CUT_t}$, there is an unique $\mathbf{y}' \in \mathscr{F}^{r_t}$ such that

$$\mathbf{y} G_t^{CUT_t} = \mathbf{y}' G_t^\rho,$$

which thus leads to a mapping ϕ_ρ from $\mathscr{C}_{CUT_t}$ to $\mathscr{F}^{r_t}$, to be specific,

$$\phi_\rho : \mathscr{C}_{CUT_t} \to \mathscr{F}^{r_t}$$
$$\mathbf{y} \mapsto \mathbf{y}'$$

with $\mathbf{y}' \in \mathscr{F}^{r_t}$ such that $\mathbf{y} G_t^{CUT_t} = \mathbf{y}' G_t^\rho$. In fact, the mapping ϕ_ρ is also an injection. Assume the contrary that there exist two distinct $\mathbf{y}_1, \mathbf{y}_2 \in \mathscr{C}_{CUT_t}$ such that

$$\mathbf{y}_1 G_t^{CUT_t} = \mathbf{y}_2 G_t^{CUT_t} = \mathbf{y}' G_t^\rho \tag{4.4}$$

for some $\mathbf{y}' \in \mathscr{F}^{r_t}$. Together with the injective property of the mapping $\text{En}^{(CUT_t)}$, there exist two distinct message vectors $\mathbf{x}_1, \mathbf{x}_2 \in \mathscr{F}^\omega$ such that $\mathbf{y}_i = \mathbf{x}_i F_{CUT_t}$, $i = 1, 2$. Thus, from (4.3),

$$\mathbf{y}_i G_t^{CUT_t} = \mathbf{x}_i F_{CUT_t} G_t^{CUT_t} = \mathbf{x}_i F_t, \; i = 1, 2. \tag{4.5}$$

Combining the equalities (4.4) and (4.5), this leads to $\mathbf{x}_1 F_t = \mathbf{x}_2 F_t$ implying $\mathbf{x}_1 = \mathbf{x}_2$ as F_t is full-rank. This is a contradiction.

Subsequently, let $\mathscr{C}_{\phi_\rho} = \{\phi_\rho(\mathbf{y}) : \text{all } \mathbf{y} \in \mathscr{C}_{CUT_t}\}$. Then $\mathscr{C}_{\phi_\rho}$ can be regarded as a classical error-correcting code with codeword length r_t and cardinality $|\mathscr{C}_{\phi_\rho}| = |\mathscr{C}_{CUT_t}| = q^\omega$. Furthermore, we claim that the minimum distance (the minimum Hamming distance) of the code $\mathscr{C}_{\phi_\rho}$ is no less than $d_{\min}^{(t)}$, i.e., $d_{\min}(\mathscr{C}_{\phi_\rho}) \geq d_{\min}^{(t)}$. To see this assume the contrary that $d_{\min}(\mathscr{C}_{\phi_\rho}) < d_{\min}^{(t)}$, that is, there exists two distinct codewords $\mathbf{y}_1'$ and $\mathbf{y}_2'$ in $\mathscr{C}_{\phi_\rho}$ satisfying $w_H(\mathbf{y}_1' - \mathbf{y}_2') < d_{\min}^{(t)}$. Since the mapping ϕ_ρ is injective, it is shown that $\mathbf{y}_i = \phi_\rho^{-1}(\mathbf{y}_i') \in \mathscr{C}_{CUT_t}$, $i = 1, 2$, are distinct, and

$$(\mathbf{y}_1 - \mathbf{y}_2)G_t^{CUT_t} = (\mathbf{y}_1' - \mathbf{y}_2')G_t^\rho.$$

Together with the injection of the encoding function $\text{En}^{(CUT_t)}$, there exists unique source message vector $\mathbf{x}_i \in \mathscr{F}^\omega$ such that

$$\text{En}^{(CUT_t)}(\mathbf{x}_i) = \mathbf{x}_i F_{CUT_t} = \mathbf{y}_i, \ i = 1, 2,$$

which leads to

$$(\mathbf{y}_1' - \mathbf{y}_2')G_t^\rho = (\mathbf{y}_1 - \mathbf{y}_2)G_t^{CUT_t} = (\mathbf{x}_1 F_{CUT_t} - \mathbf{x}_2 F_{CUT_t})G_t^{CUT_t} = \mathbf{x}_1 F_t - \mathbf{x}_2 F_t.$$

Let $\mathbf{z} \in \mathscr{F}^{|E|}$ be an error vector matching the error pattern ρ and $\mathbf{z}_\rho = \mathbf{y}_1' - \mathbf{y}_2'$, and then

$$\mathbf{z}G_t = \mathbf{z}_\rho G_t^\rho = (\mathbf{y}_1' - \mathbf{y}_2')G_t^\rho = \mathbf{x}_1 F_t - \mathbf{x}_2 F_t.$$

So the Hamming weight of $\mathbf{z}$ satisfies:

$$w_H(\mathbf{z}) = w_H(\mathbf{y}_1' - \mathbf{y}_2') < d_{\min}^{(t)}.$$

In other words, there exist an error vector $\mathbf{z}$ with $w_H(\mathbf{z}) < d_{\min}^{(t)}$ such that $\mathbf{x}_1 F_t - \mathbf{x}_2 F_t = \mathbf{z}G_t$, which shows that

$$d^{(t)}(\mathbf{x}_1 F_t, \mathbf{x}_2 F_t) \leq w_H(\mathbf{z}) < d_{\min}^{(t)}.$$

This is a contradiction. Therefore, we can say $d_{\min}(\mathscr{C}_{\phi_\rho}) \geq d_{\min}^{(t)}$.

Now, we have known that $\mathscr{C}_{\phi_\rho}$ can be regarded as a classical error-correcting code with codeword length r_t and the minimum distance no less than $d_{\min}^{(t)}$, and thus we have the following inequality from the Hamming bound for classical error-correcting codes:

$$q^\omega = |\mathscr{C}_{\phi_\rho}| \leq \frac{q^{r_t}}{\sum_{i=0}^{\tau^{(t)}} \binom{r_t}{i}(q-1)^i}, \tag{4.6}$$

and $|\mathscr{C}_{\phi_\rho}| = |\mathscr{C}_{CUT_t}| = |\mathscr{C}_t| = q^\omega$, which completes the proof. $\qquad\square$

Not difficult to see that the Hamming bound in Theorem 4.1 is a special case of this theorem. So Theorem 4.2 can also be regarded as the Hamming bound of linear network error correction codes.

In addition, let $f(n) = \frac{q^n}{\sum_{i=0}^{\tau} \binom{n}{i}(q-1)^i}$ for positive integers n and τ satisfying $n \geq 2\tau$ with $q \geq 2$. Then

$$
\begin{aligned}
\frac{f(n)}{f(n+1)} &= \frac{q^n}{\sum_{i=0}^{\tau} \binom{n}{i}(q-1)^i} \cdot \frac{\sum_{i=0}^{\tau} \binom{n+1}{i}(q-1)^i}{q^{n+1}} \\
&= \frac{\sum_{i=0}^{\tau} \left[\binom{n}{i} + \binom{n}{i-1}\right](q-1)^i}{q \sum_{i=0}^{\tau} \binom{n}{i}(q-1)^i} \\
&= \frac{\sum_{i=0}^{\tau} \binom{n}{i}(q-1)^i + \sum_{i=0}^{\tau} \binom{n}{i-1}(q-1)^i}{q \sum_{i=0}^{\tau} \binom{n}{i}(q-1)^i} \\
&= \frac{1}{q} + \frac{\sum_{i=0}^{\tau} \binom{n}{i-1}(q-1)^i}{q \sum_{i=0}^{\tau} \binom{n}{i}(q-1)^i} \\
&< \frac{1}{q} + \frac{1}{q} = \frac{2}{q} \leq 1,
\end{aligned}
\tag{4.7}
$$

where we set $\binom{n}{-1} = 0$, the first inequality in (4.7) follows from $\binom{n}{i-1} < \binom{n}{i}$ for all $i = 0, 1, 2, \cdots, \tau$ with $2\tau \leq n$, and the second inequality in (4.7) follows from $q \geq 2$. This means $f(n+1) \geq f(n)$.

Notice that we have obtained in the above proof $r_t \geq d_{\min}(\mathscr{C}_{\phi_\rho}) \geq d_{\min}^{(t)} \geq 2\tau^{(t)}$. Therefore, we can apply this result recursively, and combine it with the equality (3.3), that is, for any $e \in E$,

$$
\text{row}_t(e) = \sum_{d \in Out(head(e))} k_{e,d} \cdot \text{row}_t(d),
$$

to obtain the following corollary.

Corollary 4.1. *Consider a linear network error correction code over a network. Then the number $|\mathscr{C}_t|$ of codewords at the sink node $t \in T$ satisfies:*

$$
|\mathscr{C}_t| = q^\omega \leq \frac{q^{r_t}}{\sum_{i=0}^{\tau^{(t)}} \binom{r_t}{i}(q-1)^i},
$$

where again q is the size of the base field, ω is the information rate, $\tau^{(t)} = \lfloor (d_{\min}^{(t)} - 1)/2 \rfloor$ with $d_{\min}^{(t)}$ being the minimum distance at the sink node $t \in T$, and r_t is the dimension of the error space $\Delta(t, Out(s))$, i.e., $\dim(\Delta(t, Out(s))) = r_t$.

And in some papers such as [50], this bound is called the Hamming bound of linear network error correction codes.

4.2 Singleton Bound and Network MDS Codes

In this section, we will discuss a very important upper bound—Singleton bound for linear network error correction codes. First, we give this bound.

Theorem 4.3 (Singleton Bound). Let $d_{min}^{(t)}$ be the minimum distance of a regular linear network error correction code at the sink node $t \in T$. Then

$$d_{min}^{(t)} \leq C_t - \omega + 1 = \delta_t + 1,$$

where C_t is the minimum cut capacity between the source node s and the sink node t, i.e., $C_t = \text{mincut}(s,t)$, ω is the information rate, and $\delta_t \triangleq C_t - \omega$ is called the redundancy of t.

In order to prove this bound, we require the following lemma.

Lemma 4.1. For a regular linear network error correction code, let a channel set $\{e_1, e_2, \cdots, e_{C_t}\}$ be a minimum cut between the source node s and the sink node t with an upstream-to-downstream order (ancestral order) $e_1 \prec e_2 \prec \cdots \prec e_{C_t}$, where C_t is the minimum cut capacity between s and t. Further let an error pattern be $\rho = \{e_\omega, e_{\omega+1}, \cdots, e_{C_t}\}$, where again ω is the information rate. Then

$$\Phi(t) \cap \Delta(t, \rho) \neq \{\mathbf{0}\}.$$

Proof. Let $\mathbf{x}$ and $\mathbf{z}$ represent a source message vector and an error vector, respectively. Then, for each channel $e \in E$, we have $\tilde{U}_e = (\mathbf{x}\ \mathbf{z})\tilde{f}_e$, where $\tilde{U}_e$ is the output of e.

Since Rank $\left(\begin{bmatrix} \tilde{f}_{e_1} & \tilde{f}_{e_2} & \cdots & \tilde{f}_{e_{\omega-1}} \end{bmatrix}\right)$ is at most $(\omega - 1)$, there exists a nonzero message vector $\mathbf{x}_1$ and an error message vector $\mathbf{z}_1 = \mathbf{0}$ such that

$$\tilde{U}_{e_1} = \tilde{U}_{e_2} = \cdots = \tilde{U}_{e_{\omega-1}} = 0,$$

i.e.,

$$(\mathbf{x}_1\ \mathbf{z}_1) \begin{bmatrix} \tilde{f}_{e_1} & \tilde{f}_{e_2} & \cdots & \tilde{f}_{e_{\omega-1}} \end{bmatrix}$$
$$= (\mathbf{x}_1\ \mathbf{0}) \begin{bmatrix} \tilde{f}_{e_1} & \tilde{f}_{e_2} & \cdots & \tilde{f}_{e_{\omega-1}} \end{bmatrix}$$
$$= (\tilde{U}_{e_1}\ \tilde{U}_{e_2}\ \cdots\ \tilde{U}_{e_{\omega-1}}) = \mathbf{0}.$$

Moreover, as this code is regular, this implies

$$(\mathbf{x}_1\ \mathbf{0}) \begin{bmatrix} \tilde{f}_{e_1} & \tilde{f}_{e_2} & \cdots & \tilde{f}_{e_{C_t}} \end{bmatrix} = (\tilde{U}_{e_1}\ \tilde{U}_{e_2}\ \cdots\ \tilde{U}_{e_{C_t}}) \neq \mathbf{0}. \tag{4.8}$$

Assume the contrary that $(\tilde{U}_{e_1}\ \tilde{U}_{e_2}\ \cdots\ \tilde{U}_{e_{C_t}}) = \mathbf{0}$. And note that $\{e_1, e_2, \cdots, e_{C_t}\}$ is a minimum cut between s and t and $\mathbf{z}_1 = \mathbf{0}$. It follows that the received vector at the sink node t

$$\mathbf{y}_t = (\tilde{U}_e : e \in In(t)) = \mathbf{0},$$

which implies that $(\mathbf{x}_1 \ \mathbf{0})\tilde{F}_t = \mathbf{0}$ from the decoding equation $(\mathbf{x}_1 \ \mathbf{z}_1)\tilde{F}_t = \mathbf{y}_t$. There-fore, $\mathbf{x}_1 = \mathbf{0}$ follows from $\dim(\Phi(t)) = \omega$ because the linear network error correction code considered is regular. This contradicts our assumption $\mathbf{x}_1 \neq \mathbf{0}$.

On the other hand, for the vector $(\tilde{U}_{e_1} \ \tilde{U}_{e_2} \ \cdots \ \tilde{U}_{e_{C_t}})$ from (4.8), there exists another source message vector $\mathbf{x}_2 = \mathbf{0}$ and another error message vector $\mathbf{z}_2$ matching the error pattern $\rho = \{e_\omega, e_{\omega+1}, \cdots, e_{C_t}\}$, such that

$$(\mathbf{x}_2 \ \mathbf{z}_2) \left[\tilde{f}_{e_1} \ \tilde{f}_{e_2} \ \cdots \ \tilde{f}_{e_{C_t}} \right] = \left(\tilde{U}_{e_1} \ \tilde{U}_{e_2} \ \cdots \ \tilde{U}_{e_{C_t}} \right).$$

And note that $\mathbf{z}_2 \neq \mathbf{0}$ because $\left(\tilde{U}_{e_1} \ \tilde{U}_{e_2} \ \cdots \ \tilde{U}_{e_{C_t}} \right) \neq \mathbf{0}$. In fact, since $e_\omega \prec e_{\omega+1} \prec \cdots \prec e_{C_t}$, we can set sequentially for $e \in \rho$:

$$z_e = \tilde{U}_e - \sum_{d \in In(tail(e))} k_{d,e} \tilde{U}'_d,$$

where $\tilde{U}'_d$ is the output of channel d in this case.

Therefore, it follows that

$$(\mathbf{x}_1 \ \mathbf{0}) \ \tilde{F}_t = (\mathbf{0} \ \mathbf{z}_2) \ \tilde{F}_t.$$

And note that $\mathbf{z}_2$ matches the error pattern ρ. It is shown that $\Phi(t) \cap \Delta(t,\rho) \neq \{\mathbf{0}\}$. The lemma is proved. $\square$

It is not hard to see that Theorem 4.3 is an obvious consequence of Proposition 3.3 and Lemma 4.1. Conventionally, if a regular linear network error correction code satisfies the Singleton bound with equality, that is, $d_{\min}^{(t)} = \delta_t + 1$ for each $t \in T$, then this code is called *linear network error correction maximum distance separable (MDS) code*, or *network MDS code* for short.

In the following, we will indicate that this Singleton bound is tight, that is, there exist linear network error correction codes meeting this Singleton bound with equality. Before discussion further, we give some notation and definitions.

Definition 4.1. For an error pattern ρ and extended global encoding kernels $\tilde{f}_e$, $e \in E$,

- $\tilde{f}_e^\rho$ is an $(\omega + |\rho|)$-dimensional column vector obtained from

$$\tilde{f}_e = \left[\tilde{f}_e(d) : \ d \in In(s) \cup E \right]$$

by removing all entries $\tilde{f}_e(d)$, $d \notin In(s) \cup \rho$, and $\tilde{f}_e^\rho$ is called the extended global encoding kernel of channel e restricted to the error pattern ρ.
- f_e^ρ is an $(\omega + |E|)$-dimensional column vector obtained from

$$\tilde{f}_e = \left[\tilde{f}_e(d) : \ d \in In(s) \cup E \right]$$

by replacing all entries $\tilde{f}_e(d)$, $d \notin In(s) \cup \rho$, by 0.
- $f_e^{\rho^c}$ is an $(\omega + |E|)$-dimensional column vector obtained from

$$\tilde{f}_e = \left[\tilde{f}_e(d) : \ d \in In(s) \cup E \right]$$

by replacing all entries $\tilde{f}_e(d)$, $d \in In(s) \cup \rho$, by 0.

Note that $f_e^\rho + f_e^{\rho^c} = \tilde{f}_e$.

Example 4.1. Continue taking the network and the linear network error correction code in Example 3.1 into account. For an error pattern $\rho = \{e_3, e_7, e_9\}$, we have

$$\tilde{F}_t^\rho = \begin{bmatrix} \tilde{f}_{e_7}^\rho & \tilde{f}_{e_8}^\rho & \tilde{f}_{e_9}^\rho & \tilde{f}_{e_{10}}^\rho & \tilde{f}_{e_{11}}^\rho \end{bmatrix} = \begin{bmatrix} 3 & 5 & 4 & 7 & 1 \\ 3 & 6 & 8 & 2 & 4 \\ 1 & 2 & 2 & 4 & 0 \\ 1 & 0 & 0 & 0 & 0 \\ 0 & 0 & 1 & 0 & 0 \end{bmatrix},$$

and

$$F_t^\rho = \begin{bmatrix} f_{e_7}^\rho & f_{e_8}^\rho & f_{e_9}^\rho & f_{e_{10}}^\rho & f_{e_{11}}^\rho \end{bmatrix} = \begin{bmatrix} 3 & 5 & 4 & 7 & 1 \\ 3 & 6 & 8 & 2 & 4 \\ 0 & 0 & 0 & 0 & 0 \\ 0 & 0 & 0 & 0 & 0 \\ 1 & 2 & 2 & 4 & 0 \\ 0 & 0 & 0 & 0 & 0 \\ 0 & 0 & 0 & 0 & 0 \\ 0 & 0 & 0 & 0 & 0 \\ 1 & 0 & 0 & 0 & 0 \\ 0 & 0 & 0 & 0 & 0 \\ 0 & 0 & 0 & 0 & 0 \\ 0 & 0 & 1 & 0 & 0 \\ 0 & 0 & 0 & 0 & 0 \\ 0 & 0 & 0 & 0 & 0 \\ 0 & 0 & 0 & 0 & 0 \\ 0 & 0 & 0 & 0 & 0 \end{bmatrix}.$$

Next, we will give a constructive proof to show that the Singleton bound is tight, which then can induce an algorithm for constructing linear network error correction codes. First, we need the following lemma, and define $R_t(\delta_t)$ as the set of error patterns ρ satisfying $|\rho| = rank_t(\rho) = \delta_t$, that is,

$$R_t(\delta_t) = \{\text{error pattern } \rho : |\rho| = rank_t(\rho) = \delta_t\}.$$

Lemma 4.2. *For each sink node $t \in T$ and each error pattern $\rho \in R_t(\delta_t)$, there exist $(\omega + \delta_t)$ channel-disjoint paths from either s or ρ to t, which satisfy the properties that*

1. there are exactly δ_t paths from ρ to t, and ω paths from s to t;
2. these δ_t paths from ρ to t start with the different channels in ρ.

Proof. For each sink node $t \in T$ and each error pattern $\rho \in R_t(\delta_t)$, introduce an imaginary source node s_ρ as described in Proposition 3.1, that is, let $\rho = \{e_1, e_2,$

$\cdots, e_{\delta_t}\}$ where $e_j \in In(i_j)$ for $1 \leq j \leq \delta_t$ and define $e'_j = (s_\rho, i_j)$, and further, replace each e_j by e'_j on the network, i.e., add $e'_1, e'_2, \cdots, e'_{\delta_t}$ on the network and delete $e_1, e_2, \cdots, e_{\delta_t}$ from the network. Since ρ satisfies $|\rho| = rank_t(\rho) = \delta_t$ and Proposition 3.1, there exist δ_t channel-disjoint paths from s_ρ to t. Note that the first channels of these paths are artificial channels e'_j, $1 \leq j \leq \delta_t$, introduced to connect the heads of channels in ρ. Each of these artificial channels has a corresponding channel in ρ and all δ_t distinct artificial channels $e'_1, e'_2, \cdots, e'_{\delta_t}$ correspond to δ_t distinct channels $e_1, e_2, \cdots, e_{\delta_t}$. So replace these δ_t artificial channels by their corresponding channels in ρ, and then these paths start with all channels in ρ and still are channel-disjoint.

Further, remove all channels on the above δ_t channel-disjoint paths from the network. Considering the network with the remaining channels, the minimum cut capacity between s and t is at least $C_t - \delta_t = \omega$. Therefore, there still exist ω channel-disjoint paths from s to t, and they are also channel-disjoint with the removed δ_t paths starting with channels in ρ. This lemma is proved. $\square$

Furthermore, in Lemma 4.2, assign ω imaginary message channels $d'_1, d'_2, \cdots, d'_\omega$ to the ω paths from s to t, and assign δ_t imaginary error channels e', $e \in \rho$, to the δ_t paths from ρ to t, i.e., for each $e \in \rho$, assign e' to the path from e to t. This leads to the following corollary.

Corollary 4.2. *For each sink node $t \in T$ and each error pattern $\rho \in R_t(\delta_t)$, there exist $(\omega + \delta_t)$ channel-disjoint paths from either $In(s) = \{d'_1, d'_2, \cdots, d'_\omega\}$ or $\rho' = \{e' : e \in \rho\}$ to t, which satisfy the properties that*

1. *there are exactly δ_t paths from ρ' to t, and ω paths from $In(s)$ to t;*
2. *these δ_t paths from ρ' to t start with the distinct channels in ρ' and for each path, if it starts with $e' \in \rho'$, then it passes through the corresponding $e \in \rho$.*

The following theorem shows the attainability of the Singleton bound, and a constructive proof is given. Briefly speaking, in order to show this attainability, it suffices to prove that under the requirement of the field size, we can construct a linear network error correction code such that $\Phi(t) \cap \Delta(t, \rho) = \{0\}$ for all $t \in T$ and $\rho \in R_t(\delta_t)$, since it will be shown that any error pattern η with $rank_t(\eta) < \delta_t$ satisfies $\eta \prec_t \rho$ for some $\rho \in R_t(\delta_t)$, which implies that $\Phi(t) \cap \Delta(t, \eta) = \{0\}$. Together with the definition of the minimum distance, this leads to $d_{\min}^{(t)} = \delta_t + 1$ for all sink nodes $t \in T$.

Theorem 4.4. *If $|\mathscr{F}| \geq \sum_{t \in T} |R_t(\delta_t)|$, then there exist linear network error correction MDS codes, i.e., for all $t \in T$,*

$$d_{\min}^{(t)} = \delta_t + 1.$$

Proof. Let $G = (V, E)$ be a single source multicast network, where s is the single source, T is the set of sink nodes, $J = V - \{s\} - T$ is the set of internal nodes, and E represents the set of channels in G. Let $\tilde{G} = (\tilde{V}, \tilde{E})$ be the extended network of G. For each $t \in T$ and each $\rho \in R_t(\delta_t)$, $\mathscr{P}_{t,\rho}$ denotes a set of $(\omega + \delta_t)$ channel-disjoint paths satisfying properties 1. and 2. in Corollary 4.2. Denote by $E_{t,\rho}$ the collection of all channels on paths in $\mathscr{P}_{t,\rho}$.

Now, we define a dynamic set of channels $CUT_{t,\rho}$ for each $t \in T$ and each $\rho \in R_t(\delta_t)$, and initialize

$$CUT_{t,\rho} = In(s) \cup \rho' = \{d_1', d_2', \cdots, d_\omega'\} \cup \{e' : e \in \rho\},$$

where again e' is the imaginary error channel corresponding to e. Initialize $\tilde{f}_d = \mathbf{0}$ for all $d \in E$ and $\tilde{f}_d = 1_d$ for all $d \in In(s) \cup E'$. Naturally, we are interested in $\{\tilde{f}_d : d \in CUT_{t,\rho}\}$.

For any subset $B \subseteq In(s) \cup E' \cup E$, define four vector spaces below:

$$\tilde{\mathscr{L}}(B) = \langle\{\tilde{f}_e : e \in B\}\rangle,$$
$$\tilde{\mathscr{L}}^\rho(B) = \langle\{\tilde{f}_e^\rho : e \in B\}\rangle,$$
$$\mathscr{L}^\rho(B) = \langle\{f_e^\rho : e \in B\}\rangle,$$
$$\mathscr{L}^{\rho^c}(B) = \langle\{f_e^{\rho^c} : e \in B\}\rangle.$$

For $CUT_{t,\rho}$, note that the initial set is $CUT_{t,\rho} = In(s) \cup \rho'$, which means

$$\tilde{\mathscr{L}}(CUT_{t,\rho}) = \langle\{\tilde{f}_d : d \in In(s) \cup \rho'\}\rangle = \langle\{1_d : d \in In(s) \cup \{e' : e \in \rho\}\}\rangle.$$

Thus $[\tilde{f}_d^\rho : d \in CUT_{t,\rho}] = [\tilde{f}_d^\rho : d \in In(s) \cup \rho']$ is an identity matrix of size $(\omega + \delta_t) \times (\omega + \delta_t)$. That is,

$$\text{Rank}\left([\tilde{f}_d^\rho : d \in In(s) \cup \rho']\right) = \omega + \delta_t \text{ or } \dim(\tilde{\mathscr{L}}^\rho(CUT_{t,\rho})) = \omega + \delta_t.$$

Next, we will update $CUT_{t,\rho}$ in the ancestral order of all nodes until $CUT_{t,\rho} \subseteq In(t)$.

For each $i \in V$, consider all channels $e \in Out(i)$ in an arbitrary order. For each $e \in Out(i)$, if $e \notin \cup_{t \in T} \cup_{\rho \in R_t(\delta_t)} E_{t,\rho}$, let $\tilde{f}_e = 1_e$, and all $CUT_{t,\rho}$ remain unchanged. Otherwise $e \in \cup_{t \in T} \cup_{\rho \in R_t(\delta_t)} E_{t,\rho}$, i.e., $e \in E_{t,\rho}$ for some $t \in T$ and some $\rho \in R_t(\delta_t)$, choose

$$\tilde{g}_e \in \tilde{\mathscr{L}}(In(i) \cup \{e'\}) \setminus \cup_{t \in T} \cup_{\substack{\rho \in R_t(\delta_t): \\ e \in E_{t,\rho}}} \left[\mathscr{L}^\rho(CUT_{t,\rho} \setminus \{e(t,\rho)\}) + \mathscr{L}^{\rho^c}(In(i) \cup \{e'\})\right],$$

(4.9)

where we use $e(t,\rho)$ to denote the previous channel of e on the path which e locates on in $\mathscr{P}_{t,\rho}$, and the addition "+" represents the sum of two vector spaces. Further, let

$$\tilde{f}_e = \begin{cases} \tilde{g}_e + 1_e & \text{if } \tilde{g}_e(e) = 0, \\ \tilde{g}_e(e)^{-1} \cdot \tilde{g}_e & \text{otherwise.} \end{cases}$$

For those $CUT_{t,\rho}$ satisfying $e \in E_{t,\rho}$, update $CUT_{t,\rho} = \{CUT_{t,\rho} \setminus \{e(t,\rho)\}\} \cup \{e\}$; and for others, $CUT_{t,\rho}$ remain unchanged.

Updating all channels in E one by one as the same method, one can see that all $\tilde{f}_e, e \in E$ are well-defined and finally, $CUT_{t,\rho} \subseteq In(t)$ for all $t \in T$ and $\rho \in R_t(\delta_t)$. To complete the proof, we only need to prove the following two conclusions:

1. For each $t \in T$, $d^{(t)}_{\min} = \delta_t + 1$.
2. There exists nonzero column vector $\tilde{g}_e$ satisfying (4.9).

The proof of 1.: We will indicate that all $CUT_{t,\rho}$ satisfy $\dim(\mathscr{L}^\rho(CUT_{t,\rho})) = \omega + \delta_t$ during the whole updating process by induction.

Assume that all channels before e have been updated and $\dim(\mathscr{L}^\rho(CUT_{t,\rho})) = \omega + \delta_t$ for each $CUT_{t,\rho}$. Now, we take the channel e into account. Since we choose

$$\tilde{g}_e \in \mathscr{L}(In(i) \cup \{e'\}) \setminus \bigcup_{\substack{t \in T \\ e \in E_{t,\rho}}} \bigcup_{\rho \in R_t(\delta_t):} \left[\mathscr{L}^\rho(CUT_{t,\rho} \setminus \{e(t,\rho)\}) + \mathscr{L}^{\rho^c}(In(i) \cup \{e'\}) \right],$$

it follows that $\tilde{g}^\rho_e$ and $\{\tilde{f}^\rho_d : d \in CUT_{t,\rho} \setminus \{e(t,\rho)\}\}$ are linearly independent for any $CUT_{t,\rho}$ with $e \in E_{t,\rho}$. Conversely, suppose that $\tilde{g}^\rho_e$ and $\{\tilde{f}^\rho_d : d \in CUT_{t,\rho} \setminus \{e(t,\rho)\}\}$ are linearly dependent. This means that g^ρ_e is a linear combination of vectors in $\{f^\rho_d : d \in CUT_{t,\rho} \setminus \{e(t,\rho)\}\}$. And $g^{\rho^c}_e$ is a linear combination of vectors in $\{f^{\rho^c}_d : d \in In(i) \cup \{e'\}\}$ because of $\tilde{g}_e \in \mathscr{L}(In(i) \cup \{e'\})$. Therefore, $\tilde{g}_e = g^\rho_e + g^{\rho^c}_e$ is a linear combination of vectors in

$$\{f^\rho_d : d \in CUT_{t,\rho} \setminus \{e(t,\rho)\}\} \cup \{f^{\rho^c}_d : d \in In(i) \cup \{e'\}\}.$$

This is contradicts to the choice of $\tilde{g}_e$.

In the following, we will show that $\tilde{f}^\rho_e$ and $\{\tilde{f}^\rho_d : d \in CUT_{t,\rho} \setminus \{e(t,\rho)\}\}$ are also linearly independent.

- If $\tilde{g}_e(e) \neq 0$, then, since $\tilde{g}^\rho_e$ and $\{\tilde{f}^\rho_d : d \in CUT_{t,\rho} \setminus \{e(t,\rho)\}\}$ are linearly independent, $\tilde{f}^\rho_e = \tilde{g}_e(e)^{-1} \cdot \tilde{g}^\rho_e$ and $\{\tilde{f}^\rho_d : d \in CUT_{t,\rho} \setminus \{e(t,\rho)\}\}$ are also linearly independent.
- Otherwise $\tilde{g}_e(e) = 0$. We claim that $e \notin \rho$. Assume the contrary, i.e., $e \in \rho$. Thus $e(t,\rho) = e'$ which means $\tilde{f}_{e(t,\rho)} = 1_e$ and $\tilde{f}_d(e) = 0$ for all $d \in CUT_{t,\rho} \setminus \{e(t,\rho)\}$. Together with $\tilde{g}_e(e) = 0$ and $\dim(\mathscr{L}^\rho(CUT_{t,\rho})) = \omega + \delta_t$, it follows that $\tilde{g}^\rho_e$ is a linear combination of vectors in $\{\tilde{f}^\rho_d : d \in CUT_{t,\rho} \setminus \{e(t,\rho)\}\}$. This implies that

$$\tilde{g}_e \in \mathscr{L}^\rho(CUT_{t,\rho} \setminus \{e(t,\rho)\}) + \mathscr{L}^{\rho^c}(In(i) \cup \{e'\}),$$

which leads to a contradiction. Hence, in view of $e \notin \rho$, one obtains $\tilde{g}^\rho_e = \tilde{f}^\rho_e$, which implies that $\tilde{f}^\rho_e$ and $\{\tilde{f}^\rho_d : d \in CUT_{t,\rho} \setminus \{e(t,\rho)\}\}$ are linearly independent.

Finally, after all updates, we have $CUT_{t,\rho} \subseteq In(t)$ for each $t \in T$ and each $\rho \in R_t(\delta_t)$, and $\text{Rank}\left([\tilde{f}^\rho_e : e \in CUT_{t,\rho}]\right) = \omega + \delta_t$. Since the matrix $[\tilde{f}^\rho_e : e \in CUT_{t,\rho}]$ is a submatrix of $\tilde{F}^\rho_t = [\tilde{f}^\rho_e : e \in In(t)]$ with the same number of rows, it follows that $\text{Rank}(\tilde{F}^\rho_t) = \omega + \delta_t$, i.e., $\Phi(t) \cap \Delta(t,\rho) = \{0\}$.

For each error pattern $\eta \subseteq E$ satisfying $rank_t(\eta) < \delta_t$, there exists an error pattern $\rho \in R_t(\delta_t)$ such that $\eta \prec_t \rho$ from Proposition 3.1. This implies that $\Delta(t,\eta) \subseteq \Delta(t,\rho)$, and thus,

$$\Phi(t) \cap \Delta(t,\eta) \subsetneq \Phi(t) \cap \Delta(t,\rho) = \{0\}.$$

Now, we can say that $d_{\min}^{(t)} \geq \delta_t + 1$ for all $t \in T$, which, together with $d_{\min}^{(t)} \leq \delta_t + 1$ from Theorem 4.3, shows that $d_{\min}^{(t)} = \delta_t + 1$ for all $t \in T$.

The proof of 2.: We just need to prove that if $|\mathscr{F}| \geq \sum_{t \in T} |R_t(\delta_t)|$, then

$$\left| \tilde{\mathscr{L}}(In(i) \cup \{e'\}) \setminus \bigcup_{\substack{t \in T}} \bigcup_{\substack{\rho \in R_t(\delta_t): \\ e \in E_{t,\rho}}} \left[\mathscr{L}^\rho (CUT_{t,\rho} \setminus \{e(t,\rho)\}) + \mathscr{L}^{\rho^c}(In(i) \cup \{e'\}) \right] \right| > 0.$$

Let

$$\dim(\tilde{\mathscr{L}}(In(i) \cup \{e'\})) = k.$$

For each $t \in T$ and $\rho \in R_t(\delta_t)$, if $e \in E_{t,\rho}$, then $e(t,\rho) \in In(i) \cup \{e'\}$, that is, $\tilde{f}_{e(t,\rho)} \in \tilde{\mathscr{L}}(In(i) \cup \{e'\})$. Moreover, we know $f^\rho_{e(t,\rho)} \notin \mathscr{L}^\rho(CUT_{t,\rho} \setminus \{e(t,\rho)\})$, in other words, $f^\rho_{e(t,\rho)} \notin \mathscr{L}^\rho(CUT_{t,\rho} \setminus \{e(t,\rho)\})$, and $f^\rho_{e(t,\rho)} \notin \mathscr{L}^{\rho^c}(In(i) \cup \{e'\})$. Together with $f^{\rho^c}_{e(t,\rho)} \in \mathscr{L}^{\rho^c}(In(i) \cup \{e'\})$ and $\tilde{f}_{e(t,\rho)} = f^\rho_{e(t,\rho)} + f^{\rho^c}_{e(t,\rho)}$, this implies that

$$\tilde{f}_{e(t,\rho)} \notin \mathscr{L}^\rho(CUT_{t,\rho} \setminus \{e(t,\rho)\}) + \mathscr{L}^{\rho^c}(In(i) \cup \{e'\}).$$

Therefore,

$$\dim\left(\tilde{\mathscr{L}}(In(i) \cup \{e'\}) \cap \left[\mathscr{L}^\rho(CUT_{t,\rho} \setminus \{e(t,\rho)\}) + \mathscr{L}^{\rho^c}(In(i) \cup \{e'\}) \right] \right) \leq k - 1. \tag{4.10}$$

Consequently,

$$\left| \tilde{\mathscr{L}}(In(i) \cup \{e'\}) \setminus \bigcup_{\substack{t \in T}} \bigcup_{\substack{\rho \in R_t(\delta_t): \\ e \in E_{t,\rho}}} \left[\mathscr{L}^\rho (CUT_{t,\rho} \setminus \{e(t,\rho)\}) + \mathscr{L}^{\rho^c}(In(i) \cup \{e'\}) \right] \right|$$

$$= \left| \tilde{\mathscr{L}}(In(i) \cup \{e'\}) \right| - \left| \tilde{\mathscr{L}}(In(i) \cup \{e'\}) \right.$$

$$\left. \cap \left\{ \bigcup_{\substack{t \in T}} \bigcup_{\substack{\rho \in R_t(\delta_t): \\ e \in E_{t,\rho}}} \left[\mathscr{L}^\rho (CUT_{t,\rho} \setminus \{e(t,\rho)\}) + \mathscr{L}^{\rho^c}(In(i) \cup \{e'\}) \right] \right\} \right| \tag{4.11}$$

$$> |\mathscr{F}|^k - \sum_{t \in T} \sum_{\rho \in R_t(\delta_t)} |\mathscr{F}|^{k-1} \tag{4.12}$$

$$\geq |\mathscr{F}|^{k-1} \left[|\mathscr{F}| - \sum_{t \in T} |R_t(\delta_t)| \right]$$

$$\geq 0, \tag{4.13}$$

where the last step (4.13) follows from $|\mathscr{F}| \geq \sum_{t \in T} |R_t(\delta_t)|$. For the inequality (4.11) > (4.12), it is readily seen from (4.10) that (4.11) $\geq$ (4.12). It suffices to show (4.11) > (4.12). It is not difficult to obtain that (4.11) = (4.12), i.e.,

$$\left|\mathscr{\tilde{L}}(In(i)\cup\{e'\})\cap\{\cup_{t\in T}\cup_{\rho\in R_t(\delta_t):\atop e\in E_{t,\rho}}\left[\mathscr{L}^\rho(CUT_{t,\rho}\setminus\{e(t,\rho)\})+\mathscr{L}^{\rho^c}(In(i)\cup\{e'\})\right]\}\right|$$

$$=\sum_{t\in T}\sum_{\rho\in R_t(\delta_t)}|\mathscr{F}|^{k-1}$$

if and only if $|T|=1$, $|R_t(\delta_t)|=1$ and

$$\dim(\mathscr{\tilde{L}}(In(i)\cup\{e'\})\cap[\mathscr{L}^\rho(CUT_{t,\rho}\setminus\{e(t,\rho)\})+\mathscr{L}^{\rho^c}(In(i)\cup\{e'\})])=k-1$$

with $e\in E_{t,\rho}$, where $R_t(\delta_t)=\{\rho\}$. However, it is impossible that $|R_t(\delta_t)|=1$ because $\delta_t<C_t$. The proof is completed.   □

This constructive proof was proposed in [17, 18], and by Theorem 4.4, it is shown that the size of the required base field $\sum_{t\in T}|R_t(\delta_t)|$ is enough for the existence of network MDS codes, which is smaller than the previous results that the required size of the base field is at least $\sum_{t\in T}\binom{|E|}{\delta_t}$ in [38, 49, 50].

For any channel $e\in E$, if there exists a path from e to the sink node t, then we say that e is connective with t.

Lemma 4.3. *Let E_t be the set of channels which are connective with the sink node $t\in T$. Then*

$$\sum_{t\in T}|R_t(\delta_t)|\leq\sum_{t\in T}\binom{|E_t|}{\delta_t}\leq\sum_{t\in T}\binom{|E|}{\delta_t}.$$

Moreover, the necessary condition of the second inequality holding with equality is that there exists only one sink node in the network, i.e., $|T|=1$.

Proof. Both inequalities are clear, and we will just consider the necessary condition of the second inequality holding with equality. Suppose that there are more than one sink node, and let t and t' be two distinct sink nodes. Obviously, there exists a channel e with $head(e)=t'$. That is, e is not connective with sink node t. This implies that $|E_t|<|E|$, and thus $\binom{|E_t|}{\delta_t}<\binom{|E|}{\delta_t}$, which shows that $\sum_{t\in T}\binom{|E_t|}{\delta_t}<\sum_{t\in T}\binom{|E|}{\delta_t}$. The lemma is proved.   □

From Theorem 4.4 and Lemma 4.3, we obtain the following corollary.

Corollary 4.3. *If $|\mathscr{F}|\geq\sum_{t\in T}\binom{|E_t|}{\delta_t}$, then there exist linear network error correction MDS codes, i.e., for all $t\in T$,*

$$d_{min}^{(t)}=\delta_t+1.$$

Example 4.2. Let G be a combination network [52, p. 450][55, p. 26] with $N=6$ and $k=4$. That is, G is a single source multicast network with $N=6$ internal nodes, where there is one and only one channel from the source node s to each internal node, and arbitrary $k=4$ internal nodes are connective with one and only one sink node. This implies that there are total $\binom{6}{4}=15$ sink nodes. Thus, for G, we know that $|J|=6$, $|T|=\binom{6}{4}=15$, and $|E|=6+4\times\binom{6}{4}=66$. It is evident that the minimum cut capacity C_t between s and any sink node t is 4. For example, Fig. 4.1 shows a

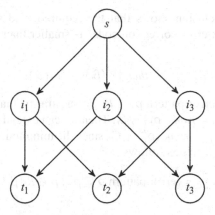

Fig. 4.1 Combination network with $N = 3, k = 2$

combination network with $N = 3$, $k = 2$. Furthermore, let the information rate be $\omega = 2$, and thus $\delta_t = 2$ for each $t \in T$. Therefore,

$$|R_t(\delta_t)| = |R_t(2)| = 4 \times \binom{4}{2} = 24$$

for each $t \in T$, and

$$\sum_{t \in T} |R_t(\delta_t)| = 15 \times 24 = 360.$$

Nevertheless,

$$\sum_{t \in T} \binom{|E_t|}{\delta_t} = 15 \times \binom{8}{2} = 420$$

and

$$\sum_{t \in T} \binom{|E|}{\delta_t} = 15 \times \binom{66}{2} = 32175.$$

Now, we take into account the general linear network error correction codes, and give the following theorem.

Theorem 4.5. *For any nonnegative integers β_t with $\beta_t \leq \delta_t$ for each $t \in T$, if $|\mathscr{F}| \geq \sum_{t \in T} |R_t(\beta_t)|$, then there exist linear network error correction codes satisfying for all $t \in T$,*

$$d_{\min}^{(t)} \geq \beta_t + 1,$$

where $R_t(\beta_t)$ is the set of error patterns ρ satisfying $|\rho| = rank_t(\rho) = \beta_t$, that is,

$$R_t(\beta_t) = \{error\ pattern\ \rho : |\rho| = rank_t(\rho) = \beta_t\}.$$

Proof. The proof of this theorem is the same as that of Theorem 4.4 so long as replace δ_t by β_t, so the details are omitted. □

The following conclusion shows that the required field size for constructing general linear network error correction codes is smaller than that for constructing network MDS codes.

Theorem 4.6. Let $\beta_t \leq \delta_t \leq \lfloor \frac{C_t}{2} \rfloor$, then $|R_t(\beta_t)| \leq |R_t(\delta_t)|$.

Proof. We choose an error pattern $\rho_1 \in R_t(\beta_t)$ arbitrarily, that is, the chosen error pattern ρ_1 satisfies $|\rho_1| = rank_t(\rho_1) = \beta_t$. Then we can extend ρ_1 to an error pattern ρ_1' with $\rho_1 \subseteq \rho_1'$ and $|\rho_1'| = rank_t(\rho_1') = C_t$, since the minimum cut capacity between s and t is C_t. Define two sets as follows:

$$\Omega_{1,\beta_t} = \{\text{error pattern } \rho \subseteq \rho_1' : \rho \in R_t(\beta_t)\}$$

and

$$\Omega_{1,\delta_t} = \{\text{error pattern } \rho' \subseteq \rho_1' : \rho' \in R_t(\delta_t)\}.$$

From the above definitions, we have

$$|\Omega_{1,\beta_t}| = \binom{C_t}{\beta_t} \text{ and } |\Omega_{1,\delta_t}| = \binom{C_t}{\delta_t}.$$

Note that $\beta_t \leq \delta_t \leq \lfloor \frac{C_t}{2} \rfloor$ implies $\binom{C_t}{\beta_t} \leq \binom{C_t}{\delta_t}$. In other words, for each $\rho \in \Omega_{1,\beta_t}$, there exists an error pattern $\rho' \in \Omega_{1,\delta_t}$ such that ρ is covered by ρ', i.e., $\rho \subseteq \rho'$, and for any distinct $\theta, \eta \in \Omega_{1,\beta_t}$, $\theta' \neq \eta'$.

Again, choose an error pattern $\rho_2 \in R_t(\beta_t)\backslash\Omega_{1,\beta_t}$ arbitrarily. In the same way as for ρ_1, the error pattern ρ_2 can be extended to an error pattern ρ_2' with $\rho_2 \subseteq \rho_2'$ and $|\rho_2'| = rank_t(\rho_2') = C_t$. Define the next two sets similarly:

$$\Omega_{2,\beta_t} = \{\text{error pattern } \rho \subseteq \rho_2' : \rho \in R_t(\beta_t), \rho \not\subseteq \rho_1' \cap \rho_2'\},$$

and

$$\Omega_{2,\delta_t} = \{\text{error pattern } \rho' \subseteq \rho_2' : \rho' \in R_t(\delta_t), \rho' \not\subseteq \rho_1' \cap \rho_2'\}.$$

Obviously, for all $\rho \in \Omega_{2,\beta_t}$ and $\rho' \in \Omega_{2,\delta_t}$, we have $\rho \notin \Omega_{1,\beta_t}$ and $\rho' \notin \Omega_{1,\delta_t}$. This means that $\Omega_{1,\beta_t} \cap \Omega_{2,\beta_t} = \emptyset$ and $\Omega_{1,\delta_t} \cap \Omega_{2,\delta_t} = \emptyset$. Let $|\rho_1' \cap \rho_2'| = k_{1,2}$. Then

$$|\Omega_{2,\beta_t}| = \binom{C_t}{\beta_t} - \binom{k_{1,2}}{\beta_t} \text{ and } |\Omega_{2,\delta_t}| = \binom{C_t}{\delta_t} - \binom{k_{1,2}}{\delta_t}.$$

We adopt the convention that $\binom{a}{b} = 0$ for $a < b$.

Similarly, we choose an error pattern $\rho_3 \in R_t(\beta_t)\backslash\Omega_{1,\beta_t} \cup \Omega_{2,\beta_t}$, and extend ρ_3 to an error pattern ρ_3' with $\rho_3 \subseteq \rho_3'$ and $|\rho_3'| = rank_t(\rho_3') = C_t$. Define

$$\Omega_{3,\beta_t} = \{\rho \subseteq \rho_3' : \rho \in R_t(\beta_t), \rho \not\subseteq \{\rho_1' \cup \rho_2'\} \cap \rho_3'\},$$

and

$$\Omega_{3,\delta_t} = \{\rho' \subseteq \rho_3' : \rho' \in R_t(\delta_t), \rho' \not\subseteq \{\rho_1' \cup \rho_2'\} \cap \rho_3'\}.$$

We claim that for all $\rho \in \Omega_{3,\beta_t}$ and $\rho' \in \Omega_{3,\delta_t}$, $\rho \notin \Omega_{1,\beta_t} \cup \Omega_{2,\beta_t}$ and $\rho' \notin \Omega_{1,\delta_t} \cup \Omega_{2,\delta_t}$. Conversely, suppose that $\rho \in \cup_{i=1}^2 \Omega_{i,\beta_t}$ (resp. $\rho' \in \cup_{i=1}^2 \Omega_{i,\delta_t}$). Together with $\rho \in \Omega_{3,\beta_t}$ (resp. $\rho' \in \Omega_{3,\delta_t}$), this shows that $\rho \subseteq \{\rho_1' \cup \rho_2'\} \cap \rho_3'$ (resp. $\rho' \subseteq \{\rho_1' \cup \rho_2'\} \cap \rho_3'$). It contradicts to our choice $\rho \in \Omega_{3,\beta_t}$. Thus, $\Omega_{3,\beta_t} \cap \Omega_{i,\beta_t} = \emptyset$ and $\Omega_{3,\delta_t} \cap \Omega_{i,\delta_t} = \emptyset$, $i = 1, 2$. Further, let $|\{\rho_1' \cup \rho_2'\} \cap \rho_3'| = k_{1,2,3}$. Then

$$|\Omega_{3,\beta_t}| = \binom{C_t}{\beta_t} - \binom{k_{1,2,3}}{\beta_t} \text{ and } |\Omega_{3,\delta_t}| = \binom{C_t}{\delta_t} - \binom{k_{1,2,3}}{\delta_t}.$$

We continue this procedure until we cannot choose a new error pattern $\rho \in R_t(\beta_t)$. Since $|R_t(\beta_t)|$ is finite, this procedure will stop at some step. Without loss of generality, assume that the procedure stops at the mth step. That is, $R_t(\beta_t) = \cup_{i=1}^m \Omega_{i,\beta_t}$. Together with what we have proved above, $\Omega_{i,\beta_t} \cap \Omega_{j,\beta_t} = \emptyset$ for all i, j satisfying $i \neq j$ ($1 \leq i, j \leq m$). This implies that

$$|R_t(\beta_t)| = \sum_{i=1}^m |\Omega_{i,\beta_t}| = \sum_{i=1}^m \left[\binom{C_t}{\beta_t} - \binom{k_{1,2,\cdots,i}}{\beta_t} \right],$$

where set $k_1 = 0$. Similarly, we also have $\Omega_{i,\delta_t} \cap \Omega_{j,\delta_t} = \emptyset$ for all i, j satisfying $i \neq j$ ($1 \leq i, j \leq m$), and $\cup_{i=1}^m \Omega_{i,\delta_t} \subseteq R_t(\delta_t)$, which implies that

$$|R_t(\delta_t)| \geq \sum_{i=1}^m |\Omega_{i,\delta_t}| = \sum_{i=1}^m \left[\binom{C_t}{\delta_t} - \binom{k_{1,2,\cdots,i}}{\delta_t} \right].$$

In order to prove $|R_t(\beta_t)| \leq |R_t(\delta_t)|$, it suffices to show $|\Omega_{i,\beta_t}| \leq |\Omega_{i,\delta_t}|$, i.e.,

$$\binom{C_t}{\beta_t} - \binom{k_{1,2,\cdots,i}}{\beta_t} \leq \binom{C_t}{\delta_t} - \binom{k_{1,2,\cdots,i}}{\delta_t}$$

for each $i = 1, 2, \cdots, m$.

To simplify the notation, we omit the subscripts in the following discussion. It follows that we just need to prove

$$\binom{C}{\delta} - \binom{k}{\delta} \geq \binom{C}{\beta} - \binom{k}{\beta},$$

that is,

$$\binom{C}{\delta} - \binom{C}{\beta} \geq \binom{k}{\delta} - \binom{k}{\beta}, \tag{4.14}$$

where $\beta \leq \delta \leq \lfloor \frac{C}{2} \rfloor$ and $k \leq C$.

If $k < \delta$, the inequality (4.14) immediately holds. Otherwise $k \geq \delta$, note that

$$\binom{C}{\delta} - \binom{C}{\beta}$$

$$= \left[\binom{C}{\delta} - \binom{C}{\delta-1} \right] + \left[\binom{C}{\delta-1} - \binom{C}{\delta-2} \right] + \cdots$$

$$+ \left[\binom{C}{\beta+2} - \binom{C}{\beta+1} \right] + \left[\binom{C}{\beta+1} - \binom{C}{\beta} \right],$$

and

$$\binom{k}{\delta} - \binom{k}{\beta}$$

$$= \left[\binom{k}{\delta} - \binom{k}{\delta-1} \right] + \left[\binom{k}{\delta-1} - \binom{k}{\delta-2} \right] + \cdots$$

$$+ \left[\binom{k}{\beta+2} - \binom{k}{\beta+1} \right] + \left[\binom{k}{\beta+1} - \binom{k}{\beta} \right].$$

This implies that the inequality (4.14) holds provided that we can show

$$\binom{C}{a+1} - \binom{C}{a} \geq \binom{k}{a+1} - \binom{k}{a}$$

for any a satisfying $\beta \leq a \leq \delta - 1$. After a simple calculation, it is equivalent to prove

$$C(C-1)\cdots(C-a+1)(C-2a-1) \geq k(k-1)\cdots(k-a+1)(k-2a-1). \quad (4.15)$$

It is not difficult to see that the inequality (4.15) holds for all k satisfying $C \geq k \geq \delta$. This completes the proof.   □

4.3 Construction of Linear Network Error Correction MDS Codes

As discussed above, network MDS codes are optimal for network error correction as they satisfy the Singleton bound with equality. In this section, several algorithms for constructing network MDS codes are presented and analyzed in detail.

4.3.1 The First Algorithm

By the constructive proof of Theorem 4.4 in the last section, an algorithm is proposed for constructing a linear network error correction code with required error correction capability, particularly, it can be used to construct network MDS codes. In the following Algorithm 2, we will describe this constructive approach.

Algorithm 2 The algorithm for constructing a linear network error correction code with error correction capacity $d_{\min}^{(t)} \geq \beta_t$ for each $t \in T$

Input: The single source multicast network $G = (V, E)$, the information rate $\omega \leq \min_{t \in T} C_t$, and the nonnegative integer $\beta_t \leq \delta_t$ for each $t \in T$.
Output: Extended global kernels (forming a linear network error correction code).
Initialization:

1. For each $t \in T$ and each $\rho \in R_t(\beta_t)$, find $(\omega + \beta_t)$ channel-disjoint paths from $In(s)$ or ρ' to t satisfying Corollary 4.2, and use $\mathscr{P}_{t,\rho}$ to denote the set of them;
2. For each $t \in T$ and each $\rho \in R_t(\beta_t)$, initialize dynamic channel sets:

$$CUT_{t,\rho} = In(s) \cup \rho' = \{d_1', d_2', \cdots, d_\omega'\} \cup \{e' : e \in \rho\},$$

and the extended global encoding kernels $\tilde{f}_e = 1_e$ for all imaginary channels $e \in In(s) \cup E'$.

  for each node $i \in V$ (according to the given ancestral order of nodes) **do**
    for each channel $e \in Out(i)$ (according to an arbitrary order) **do**
      if $e \notin \cup_{t \in T} \cup_{\rho \in R_t(\beta_t)} E_{t,\rho}$ **then**
        $\tilde{f}_e = 1_e$,
        all $CUT_{t,\rho}$ remain unchanged.
      else if $e \in \cup_{t \in T} \cup_{\rho \in R_t(\beta_t)} E_{t,\rho}$ **then**
        choose $\tilde{g}_e \in \tilde{\mathscr{L}}(In(i) \cup \{e'\}) \setminus \cup_{t \in T} \cup_{\substack{\rho \in R_t(\beta_t): \\ e \in E_{t,\rho}}} [\mathscr{L}^\rho(CUT_{t,\rho} \setminus \{e(t,\rho)\}) + \mathscr{L}^{\rho^c}(In(i) \cup \{e'\})]$,
        if $\tilde{g}_e(e) = 0$ **then**
          $\tilde{f}_e = \tilde{g}_e + 1_e$,
        else
          $\tilde{f}_e = \tilde{g}_e(e)^{-1} \cdot \tilde{g}_e$.
        end if
        For those $CUT_{t,\rho}$ satisfying $e \in E_{t,\rho}$, update $CUT_{t,\rho} = \{CUT_{t,\rho} \setminus \{e(t,\rho)\}\} \cup \{e\}$; and for others, $CUT_{t,\rho}$ remain unchanged.
      end if
    end for
  end for

Remark 4.1. Similar to the polynomial-time Algorithm 1 for constructing linear network codes in Chap. 1, this algorithm is a greedy one, too. The verification of Algorithm 2 is from the proof of Theorems 4.4 and 4.5. In particular, if we choose $\beta_t = \delta_t$ for all $t \in T$, then, by the proposed algorithm, we can construct a linear network error correction code that meets the Singleton bound with equality. That is, we can obtain a linear network error correction MDS code. On the other hand, if we choose $\beta_t = 0$ for each $t \in T$, then this algorithm degenerates into one for constructing linear network codes and the required field size is $\sum_{t \in T} |R_t(\beta_t)| = \sum_{t \in T} |R_t(0)| = |T|$ as is well known.

As an example, we will apply Algorithm 2 to construct a network MDS code for a very simple network G_1 shown by Fig. 4.2.

Example 4.3. For the network G_1 shown by Fig. 4.2, let the topological order of all nodes be $s \prec i \prec t$, and the topological order of all channels be $e_1 \prec e_2 \prec e_3$. It is obvious that $C_t = 2$. Let $\omega = 1$, and thus $\delta_t = C_t - \omega = 1$. Furthermore, we have

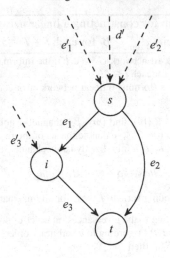

Fig. 4.2 Network G_1

$$R_t(\delta_t) = R_t(1) = \{\rho_1 = \{e_1\}, \rho_2 = \{e_2\}, \rho_3 = \{e_3\}\},$$

and

$$\mathscr{P}_{t,\rho_1} = \{P_{t,\rho_1}^{(\delta_t)} = (e_1', e_1, e_3), P_{t,\rho_1}^{(\omega)} = (d', e_2)\}, E_{t,\rho_1} = \{d', e_1', e_1, e_2, e_3\};$$

$$\mathscr{P}_{t,\rho_2} = \{P_{t,\rho_2}^{(\delta_t)} = (e_2', e_2), P_{t,\rho_2}^{(\omega)} = (d', e_1, e_3)\}, E_{t,\rho_2} = \{d', e_2', e_1, e_2, e_3\};$$

$$\mathscr{P}_{t,\rho_3} = \{P_{t,\rho_3}^{(\delta_t)} = (e_3', e_3), P_{t,\rho_3}^{(\omega)} = (d', e_2)\}, E_{t,\rho_3} = \{d', e_3', e_2, e_3\}.$$

Let the base field be $\mathbb{F}_3$. Initialize the dynamic channel sets $CUT_{t,\rho_1} = \{d', e_1'\}$, $CUT_{t,\rho_2} = \{d', e_2'\}$, $CUT_{t,\rho_3} = \{d', e_3'\}$, and

$$\tilde{f}_{d'} = \begin{bmatrix} 1 \\ 0 \\ 0 \\ 0 \end{bmatrix}, \tilde{f}_{e_1'} = \begin{bmatrix} 0 \\ 1 \\ 0 \\ 0 \end{bmatrix}, \tilde{f}_{e_2'} = \begin{bmatrix} 0 \\ 0 \\ 1 \\ 0 \end{bmatrix}, \tilde{f}_{e_3'} = \begin{bmatrix} 0 \\ 0 \\ 0 \\ 1 \end{bmatrix},$$

which leads to $\dim(\mathscr{L}^{\rho_i}(CUT_{t,\rho_i})) = 2$, $i = 1, 2, 3$.

For the channel $e_1 \in Out(s)$, $e_1 \in E_{t,\rho_1} \cap E_{t,\rho_2}$ and

$$\mathscr{L}(\{d', e_1'\}) \backslash [\mathscr{L}^{\rho_1}(\{d'\}) + \mathscr{L}^{\rho_1^c}(\{d', e_1'\})] \cup [\mathscr{L}^{\rho_2}(\{e_2'\}) + \mathscr{L}^{\rho_2^c}(\{d', e_1'\})]$$

$$= \left\langle \begin{bmatrix} 1 \\ 0 \\ 0 \\ 0 \end{bmatrix}, \begin{bmatrix} 0 \\ 1 \\ 0 \\ 0 \end{bmatrix} \right\rangle \backslash \left\langle \begin{bmatrix} 1 \\ 0 \\ 0 \\ 0 \end{bmatrix} \right\rangle \cup \left\langle \begin{bmatrix} 0 \\ 1 \\ 0 \\ 0 \end{bmatrix} \right\rangle + \left\langle \begin{bmatrix} 0 \\ 1 \\ 0 \\ 0 \end{bmatrix} \right\rangle.$$

So we choose $\tilde{g}_{e_1} = \begin{bmatrix} 1 \\ 1 \\ 0 \\ 0 \end{bmatrix}$ because of

$$\tilde{g}_{e_1} \in \mathscr{L}(\{d', e_1'\}) \backslash [\mathscr{L}^{\rho_1}(\{d'\}) + \mathscr{L}^{\rho_1^c}(\{d', e_1'\})] \cup [\mathscr{L}^{\rho_2}(\{e_2'\}) + \mathscr{L}^{\rho_2^c}(\{d', e_1'\})].$$

And $\tilde{f}_{e_1} = \tilde{g}_{e_1}$, since $\tilde{g}_{e_1}(e_1) = 1$. Then update $CUT_{t,\rho_1} = \{d', e_1\}$, $CUT_{t,\rho_2} = \{e_1, e_2'\}$, and CUT_{t,ρ_3} remains unchanged.

For the channel $e_2 \in Out(s)$, $e_2 \in E_{t,\rho_1} \cap E_{t,\rho_2} \cap E_{t,\rho_3}$ and

$$\tilde{\mathscr{L}}(\{d', e_2'\}) \backslash [\mathscr{L}^{\rho_1}(\{e_1\}) + \mathscr{L}^{\rho_1^c}(\{d', e_2'\})]$$
$$\cup [\mathscr{L}^{\rho_2}(\{e_1\}) + \mathscr{L}^{\rho_2^c}(\{d', e_2'\})] \cup [\mathscr{L}^{\rho_3}(\{e_3'\}) + \mathscr{L}^{\rho_3^c}(\{d', e_2'\})]$$

$$= \left\langle \begin{bmatrix} 1 \\ 0 \\ 0 \\ 0 \end{bmatrix}, \begin{bmatrix} 0 \\ 0 \\ 1 \\ 0 \end{bmatrix} \right\rangle \backslash \left\langle \begin{bmatrix} 1 \\ 0 \\ 0 \\ 0 \end{bmatrix} \right\rangle + \left\langle \begin{bmatrix} 0 \\ 0 \\ 1 \\ 0 \end{bmatrix} \right\rangle \cup \left\langle \begin{bmatrix} 1 \\ 0 \\ 0 \\ 0 \end{bmatrix} \right\rangle \cup \left\langle \begin{bmatrix} 0 \\ 0 \\ 0 \\ 1 \end{bmatrix} \right\rangle + \left\langle \begin{bmatrix} 0 \\ 0 \\ 1 \\ 0 \end{bmatrix} \right\rangle.$$

We choose $\tilde{g}_{e_2} = \begin{bmatrix} 1 \\ 0 \\ 1 \\ 0 \end{bmatrix}$, since

$$\tilde{g}_{e_2} \in \tilde{\mathscr{L}}(\{d', e_2'\}) \backslash [\mathscr{L}^{\rho_1}(\{e_1\}) + \mathscr{L}^{\rho_1^c}(\{d', e_2'\})]$$
$$\cup [\mathscr{L}^{\rho_2}(\{e_1\}) + \mathscr{L}^{\rho_2^c}(\{d', e_2'\})] \cup [\mathscr{L}^{\rho_3}(\{e_3'\}) + \mathscr{L}^{\rho_3^c}(\{d', e_2'\})],$$

which, together with $\tilde{g}_{e_2}(e_2) = 1$, shows that $\tilde{f}_{e_2} = \tilde{g}_{e_2}$. Then, update $CUT_{t,\rho_1} = \{e_2, e_1\}$, $CUT_{t,\rho_2} = \{e_1, e_2\}$, and $CUT_{t,\rho_3} = \{e_2, e_3'\}$.

For the channel $e_3 \in Out(i)$, $e_3 \in E_{t,\rho_1} \cap E_{t,\rho_2} \cap E_{t,\rho_3}$ and

$$\tilde{\mathscr{L}}(\{e_1, e_3'\}) \backslash [\mathscr{L}^{\rho_1}(\{e_2\}) + \mathscr{L}^{\rho_1^c}(\{e_1, e_3'\})]$$
$$\cup [\mathscr{L}^{\rho_2}(\{e_2\}) + \mathscr{L}^{\rho_2^c}(\{e_1, e_3'\})] \cup [\mathscr{L}^{\rho_3}(\{e_2\}) + \mathscr{L}^{\rho_3^c}(\{e_1, e_3'\})]$$

$$= \left\langle \begin{bmatrix} 1 \\ 1 \\ 0 \\ 0 \end{bmatrix}, \begin{bmatrix} 0 \\ 0 \\ 0 \\ 1 \end{bmatrix} \right\rangle \backslash \left\langle \begin{bmatrix} 0 \\ 0 \\ 0 \\ 1 \end{bmatrix} \right\rangle + \left\langle \begin{bmatrix} 0 \\ 0 \\ 0 \\ 1 \end{bmatrix} \right\rangle \cup \left\langle \begin{bmatrix} 0 \\ 1 \\ 0 \\ 0 \end{bmatrix} \right\rangle + \left\langle \begin{bmatrix} 1 \\ 0 \\ 0 \\ 0 \end{bmatrix}, \begin{bmatrix} 0 \\ 0 \\ 0 \\ 1 \end{bmatrix} \right\rangle \cup \left\langle \begin{bmatrix} 0 \\ 1 \\ 0 \\ 0 \end{bmatrix} \right\rangle + \left\langle \begin{bmatrix} 0 \\ 0 \\ 1 \\ 0 \end{bmatrix} \right\rangle.$$

We select $\tilde{g}_{e_3} = \begin{bmatrix} 1 \\ 1 \\ 0 \\ 1 \end{bmatrix}$ satisfying

$$\tilde{g}_{e_3} \in \tilde{\mathscr{L}}(\{e_1, e_3'\}) \backslash [\mathscr{L}^{\rho_1}(\{e_2\}) + \mathscr{L}^{\rho_1^c}(\{e_1, e_3'\})]$$
$$\cup [\mathscr{L}^{\rho_2}(\{e_2\}) + \mathscr{L}^{\rho_2^c}(\{e_1, e_3'\})] \cup [\mathscr{L}^{\rho_3}(\{e_2\}) + \mathscr{L}^{\rho_3^c}(\{e_1, e_3'\})].$$

It follows that $\tilde{f}_{e_3} = \tilde{g}_{e_3}$ from $\tilde{g}_{e_3}(e_3) = 1$, and update

$$CUT_{t,\rho_1} = CUT_{t,\rho_2} = CUT_{t,\rho_3} = \{e_2, e_3\} \subseteq In(t).$$

Consequently, the decoding matrix at t is $\tilde{F}_t = [\tilde{f}_{e_2} \ \tilde{f}_{e_3}] = \begin{bmatrix} 1 & 1 \\ 0 & 1 \\ 1 & 0 \\ 0 & 1 \end{bmatrix}$. It is easy to check that $\Phi(t) \cap \Delta(t, \rho_i) = \{0\}$ for $i = 1, 2, 3$. Further, let $\rho = \{e_1, e_2\}$, and then we have $rank_t(\rho) = 2$ and $\Phi(t) \cap \Delta(t, \rho) \neq \{0\}$, which means $d_{\min}^{(t)} = 2 = \delta_t + 1$. That is, $\{\tilde{f}_{e_1}, \tilde{f}_{e_2}, \tilde{f}_{e_3}\}$ forms a global description of an one-dimensional $\mathbb{F}_3$-valued linear network error correction MDS code for the network G_1.

Next, we will analyze the time complexity of the proposed algorithm. First, from [25], we can determine $R_t(\beta_t)$ and find $(\omega + \beta_t)$ channel-disjoint paths satisfying

Lemma 4.2 in time $\mathcal{O}(\sum_{t\in T} \binom{|E|}{\beta_t}(\omega+\beta_t)|E|)$. Both methods presented by Jaggi et al. [25] are used to analyze the time complexity of the main loop.

- If we use the method of Testing Linear Independent Quickly [25, III,A] (briefly speaking, choose a vector randomly, and then test its linear independence on other vectors), the expected time complexity is at most

$$\mathcal{O}\left(|E|\left[\sum_{t\in T}|R_t(\beta_t)|(\omega+\beta_t)(\omega+\frac{|E|+1}{2})\right]\right).$$

After a simple calculation, the total expected time complexity of the algorithm using the method of Testing Linear Independent Quickly is at most

$$\mathcal{O}\left(|E|\sum_{t\in T}(\omega+\beta_t)\cdot\left[\binom{|E|}{\beta_t}+|R_t(\beta_t)|(\omega+\frac{|E|+1}{2})\right]\right).$$

- If we use the method of Deterministic Implementation [25, III,B] (briefly speaking, use a deterministic method for choosing a vector which is linear independence on other vectors), the time complexity of the main loop is at most

$$\mathcal{O}\left(|E|\sum_{t\in T}|R_t(\beta_t)|\cdot(\omega+\beta_t)\left[\sum_{t\in T}|R_t(\beta_t)|+\omega+\beta_t\right]\right).$$

Therefore, the total time complexity of the algorithm using the method of Deterministic Implementation is at most

$$\mathcal{O}\left(|E|\sum_{t\in T}(\omega+\beta_t)\cdot\left[|R_t(\beta_t)|\left(\sum_{t\in T}|R_t(\beta_t)|+\omega+\beta_t\right)+\binom{|E|}{\beta_t}\right]\right).$$

4.3.2 The Second Algorithm

In [49, 50], Yang et al. also propose two algorithms for constructing linear network error correction MDS codes. Below we will discuss them in detail.

The first constructive method designs local encoding kernel at the source node and local encoding kernels at all internal nodes separately. To be specific, for given local encoding kernels at all internal nodes, an efficient approach is proposed to find local encoding kernel, which meets some conditions, at the source node. The following theorem and its proof describe this approach.

Theorem 4.7. *Let*

$$F_{s,t} \triangleq A_{Out(s)}FA_{In(t)}^{\top} = A_{Out(s)}(I-K)^{-1}A_{In(t)}^{\top}.$$

For all sink nodes $t \in T$, given a set of local encoding kernels with $r_t = \text{Rank}(F_{s,t})$ over a finite field $\mathscr{F}$ of size q, for every $0 \leq \omega \leq \min_{t\in T} r_t$, there exists a local encoding kernel K_s at the source node s which is an $\omega \times n_s$ matrix with rank ω such that

$$d_{\min}^{(t)} = r_t - \omega + 1, \qquad (4.16)$$

provided that q is sufficiently large, where $n_s = |Out(s)|$.

Proof. We start with any given set of local encoding kernels at all internal nodes, which determines r_t for all sink nodes $t \in T$. Fix an ω satisfying $0 \leq \omega \leq \min_{t \in T} r_t$ for each sink node t. We will then construct a local encoding kernel K_s at the source node s, which, together with the given set of local encoding kernels at all internal nodes, constitutes a linear network error correction code that satisfy (4.16) for all t.

We now construct ω vectors $g_1, g_2, \cdots, g_\omega \in \mathscr{F}^{n_s}$ as ω row vectors of K_s. Let $g_1, g_2, \cdots, g_\omega \in \mathscr{F}^{n_s}$ be a sequence of vectors derived successively as follows. For $i = 1$, choose g_1 such that for each sink node t

$$g_1 \notin \Delta_t(0, r_t - \omega), \qquad (4.17)$$

and for each i, $2 \leq i \leq \omega$, choose g_i such that for each sink node t,

$$g_i \notin \Delta_t(0, r_t - \omega) + \langle g_1, g_2, \cdots, g_{i-1} \rangle, \qquad (4.18)$$

where

$$\Delta_t(0, r_t - \omega)$$
$$= \{g : g \in \mathscr{F}^{n_s} \text{ satisfying } \min\{w_H(z) : z \in \mathscr{F}^{|E|} \text{ such that } gF_{s,t} = zG_t\} \leq r_t - \omega\}.$$

This implies

$$\Delta_t(0, r_t - \omega) \cap \langle g_1, g_2, \cdots, g_\omega \rangle = \{0\}$$

for each sink node t. If such $g_1, g_2, \cdots, g_\omega$ exist, then we claim:

- $g_1, g_2, \cdots, g_\omega$ are linearly independent;
- $d_{\min}^{(t)} \geq r_t - \omega + 1$ for each sink node $t \in T$.

The first conclusion is obvious, since $g_i \notin \langle g_1, g_2, \cdots, g_{i-1} \rangle$ for $i = 1, 2, \cdots, \omega$ from (4.17) and (4.18). In the following, we will prove the second conclusion, that is, $d_{\min}^{(t)} \geq r_t - \omega + 1$ for each sink $t \in T$.

Assume the contrary that $d_{\min}^{(t)} < r_t - \omega + 1$, or equivalently, $d_{\min}^{(t)} \leq r_t - \omega$ for some sink node t. Now, we know that the local encoding kernel at the source node is $K_s = \begin{bmatrix} g_1^\top & g_2^\top & \cdots & g_\omega^\top \end{bmatrix}^\top$, which is full-rank and of size $\omega \times n_s$. And at this time, the codebook with respect to the sink node $t \in T$ is

$$\mathscr{C}_t = \{xF_t : \text{ all } x \in \mathscr{F}^\omega\} = \{xK_sF_{s,t} : \text{ all } x \in \mathscr{F}^\omega\},$$

where note that $F_t = K_sF_{s,t}$. Further, there exist two distinct codewords $x_1F_t, x_2F_t \in \mathscr{C}_t$ satisfying $d^{(t)}(x_1F_t, x_2F_t) = d_{\min}^{(t)}$, i.e.,

$$\min\{w_H(z) : z \in \mathscr{F}^{|E|} \text{ such that } (x_1 - x_2)F_t = (x_1K_s - x_2K_s)F_{s,t} = zG_t\} = d_{\min}^{(t)}.$$

Similar to $\Delta_t(\mathbf{0}, r_t - \omega)$, for any positive integer d, we defined as

$$\Delta_t(\mathbf{0}, d)$$
$$= \{\mathbf{g} : \mathbf{g} \in \mathscr{F}^{n_s} \text{ satisfying } \min\{w_H(\mathbf{z}) : \mathbf{z} \in \mathscr{F}^{|E|} \text{ such that } \mathbf{z}G_t = \mathbf{g}F_{s,t}\} \le d\}.$$

So we have $\mathbf{0} \ne \mathbf{x}_1 K_s - \mathbf{x}_2 K_s \in \Delta_t(\mathbf{0}, d_{\min}^{(t)})$, which, together with $\Delta_t(\mathbf{0}, d_{\min}^{(t)}) \subseteq \Delta_t(\mathbf{0}, r_t - \omega)$ as the hypothesis $d_{\min}^{(t)} \le r_t - \omega$, leads to

$$\mathbf{0} \ne \mathbf{x}_1 K_s - \mathbf{x}_2 K_s \in \Delta_t(\mathbf{0}, r_t - \omega).$$

On the other hand, clearly,

$$\mathbf{0} \ne \mathbf{x}_1 K_s - \mathbf{x}_2 K_s = (\mathbf{x}_1 - \mathbf{x}_2)K_s = (\mathbf{x}_1 - \mathbf{x}_2)\begin{bmatrix} \mathbf{g}_1^\top & \mathbf{g}_2^\top & \cdots & \mathbf{g}_\omega^\top \end{bmatrix}^\top \in \langle \mathbf{g}_1, \mathbf{g}_2, \cdots, \mathbf{g}_\omega \rangle.$$

Hence,

$$\langle \mathbf{g}_1, \mathbf{g}_2, \cdots, \mathbf{g}_\omega \rangle \cap \Delta_t(\mathbf{0}, r_t - \omega) \ne \{\mathbf{0}\},$$

which is a contradiction. Therefore, we can claim $d_{\min}^{(t)} \ge r_t - \omega + 1$, which, together with the fact $d_{\min}^{(t)} \le r_t - \omega + 1$, shows $d_{\min}^{(t)} = r_t - \omega + 1$.

At the end, we show $\mathbf{g}_i$ satisfying (4.17) or (4.18) exists for all $1 \le i \le \omega$, provided the field size is sufficiently large. Observe that

$$|\Delta_t(\mathbf{0}, r_t - \omega) + \langle \mathbf{g}_1, \mathbf{g}_2, \cdots, \mathbf{g}_{i-1} \rangle| \le |\Delta_t(\mathbf{0}, r_t - \omega)| q^{i-1}. \tag{4.19}$$

Note that $\{\mathbf{g}F_{s,t} : \text{ all } \mathbf{g} \in \mathscr{F}^{n_s}\}$ constitutes a r_t-dimensional vector space since $\text{Rank}(F_{s,t}) = r_t$. Thus for any $\mathbf{g} \in \mathscr{F}^{n_s}$,

$$|\{\mathbf{g}' \in \mathscr{F}^{n_s} : \mathbf{g}' \text{ satisfying } \mathbf{g}'F_{s,t} = \mathbf{g}F_{s,t}\}| = q^{n_s - r_t}.$$

Hence,

$$|\Delta_t(\mathbf{0}, r_t - \omega)|$$
$$= |\{\mathbf{g} : \mathbf{g} \in \mathscr{F}^{n_s} \text{ satisfying } \min\{w_H(\mathbf{z}) : \mathbf{z} \in \mathscr{F}^{|E|} \text{ such that } \mathbf{z}G_t = \mathbf{g}F_{s,t}\} \le r_t - \omega\}.$$
$$= |\{\mathbf{g} : \mathbf{g} \in \mathscr{F}^{n_s} \text{ and } \exists \, \mathbf{z} \in \mathscr{F}^{|E|} \text{ with } w_H(\mathbf{z}) \le r_t - \omega \text{ such that } \mathbf{z}G_t = \mathbf{g}F_{s,t}\}|$$
$$= |\{\mathbf{g}' \in \mathscr{F}^{n_s} : \mathbf{g}' \text{ satisfying } \mathbf{g}'F_{s,t} = \mathbf{g}F_{s,t}\}|$$
$$\cdot |\{\mathbf{g}F_{s,t} : \mathbf{g} \in \mathscr{F}^{n_s} \text{ and } \exists \, \mathbf{z} \in \mathscr{F}^{|E|} \text{ with } w_H(\mathbf{z}) \le r_t - \omega \text{ such that } \mathbf{z}G_t = \mathbf{g}F_{s,t}\}|$$
$$= q^{n_s - r_t} |\{\mathbf{g}F_{s,t} : \mathbf{g} \in \mathscr{F}^{n_s}\} \cap \{\mathbf{z}G_t : \mathbf{z} \in \mathscr{F}^{|E|} \text{ and } w_H(\mathbf{z}) \le r_t - \omega\}|$$
$$\le q^{n_s - r_t} |\{\mathbf{z}G_t : \mathbf{z} \in \mathscr{F}^{|E|} \text{ and } w_H(\mathbf{z}) \le r_t - \omega\}|$$
$$\le q^{n_s - r_t} \binom{|E|}{r_t - \omega} q^{r_t - \omega} = \binom{|E|}{r_t - \omega} q^{n_s - \omega}. \tag{4.20}$$

Further, combining (4.19) and (4.20), it follows

$$|\Delta_t(\mathbf{0}, r_t - \omega) + \langle \mathbf{g}_1, \mathbf{g}_2, \cdots, \mathbf{g}_{i-1} \rangle| \le \binom{|E|}{r_t - \omega} q^{n_s - \omega + i - 1}.$$

Therefore, if $q^{n_s} > \binom{|E|}{r_t-\omega} q^{n_s-\omega+i-1}$ for all $1 \le i \le \omega$, or equivalently, $q > \binom{|E|}{r_t-\omega}$, then there exists ω vectors that can be chosen as $\mathbf{g}_i$ for $i = 1, 2, \cdots, \omega$ satisfying (4.18).

Considering all sink nodes, we have at most $\sum_{t \in T} \binom{|E|}{r_t-\omega} q^{n_s-\omega+i-1}$ vectors cannot be chosen as $\mathbf{g}_i$ for $1 \le i \le \omega$. Thus, if $q > \sum_{t \in T} \binom{|E|}{r_t-\omega}$, then there exists a vector that can be chosen as $\mathbf{g}_i$ satisfying (4.18) for each $i = 1, 2, \cdots, \omega$. This completes the proof. □

Actually, after local encoding kernels at all internal nodes are given, the above proof indicates an approach to find the proper local encoding kernel at the source node. Further if $\text{Rank}(F_{s,t}) = C_t$ for each sink node, then this approach can find a local encoding kernel at the source node such that all local encoding kernels consist of a local description of a linear network error correction MDS code.

Thus the remaining problem is to design local encoding kernels at all internal nodes such that $\text{Rank}(F_{s,t}) = C_t$ for each sink node $t \in T$. We know that Jaggi-Sanders algorithm mentioned in Chap. 1 can construct linear network codes from the source node s to each sink $t \in T$. But it is not feasible to be utilized it directly. To be specific, this algorithm constructs global encoding kernels of all channels one by one including all outgoing channels of the source node. In other words, it designs the matrix $M \triangleq [f_e : e \in E]$. Further, each sink node t can use the corresponding decoding matrix:

$$F_t = M A^\top_{In(t)} = [f_e : e \in In(t)].$$

And it is evident that

$$F_t = M \cdot A^\top_{In(t)} = K_s \cdot A_{Out(s)} \cdot (I - K)^{-1} \cdot A^\top_{In(t)} = K_s \cdot F_{s,t}, \qquad (4.21)$$

This approach for constructing linear network error correction codes needs to derive a set of local encoding kernels which can leads to $\text{Rank}(F_{s,t}) = C_t$ for each sink node $t \in T$. But, it is not feasible to obtain matrices $F_{s,t}$ with $\text{Rank}(F_{s,t}) = C_t$ from (4.21) for each sink node $t \in T$. But we may modify the Jaggi-Sanders algorithm in order to achieve the requirements, that is, constructs a set of local encoding kernels at all internal nodes satisfying $\text{Rank}(F_{s,t}) = C_t$ for each $t \in T$.

Finally, when we assume that local encoding kernels at all internal nodes are given and satisfy $\text{Rank}(F_{s,t}) = C_t$ for each sink node $t \in T$, the following Algorithm 3 completes the last step for constructing a linear network error correction MDS code.

By the discussion as above, the Algorithm 3 needs a base field of size no less than $\sum_{t \in T} \binom{|E|}{C_t-\omega} = \sum_{t \in T} \binom{|E|}{\delta_t}$ to construct a linear network error correction MDS code. And the time complexity of the Algorithm 3 is:

$$\mathcal{O}\left(\omega n_s \sum_{t \in T} \binom{|E|}{\delta_t} \left[n_s^2 + \sum_{t \in T} \binom{|E|}{\delta_t} \right] \right).$$

Algorithm 3 Construct local encoding kernel at the source node s to obtain linear network error correction MDS codes

Input: The single source multicast network $G = (V, E)$, the information rate $\omega \leq \min_{t \in T} C_t$, and the local encoding kernels at all internal nodes such that $\mathrm{Rank}(F_{s,t}) = C_t$ for each sink node $t \in T$.
Output: The local encoding kernel at the source node s such that the linear network error correction code is MDS.

1: **for each** $i = 1, 2, \cdots, \omega$ **do**
2:    find $\mathbf{g}_i$ such that $\mathbf{g}_i \notin \Delta_t(\mathbf{0}, C_t - \omega) + \langle \mathbf{g}_1, \mathbf{g}_2, \cdots, \mathbf{g}_{i-1} \rangle$ for all sink nodes $t \in T$, particularly, $\mathbf{g}_1 \notin \Delta_t(\mathbf{0}, C_t - \omega)$ for all sink nodes $t \in T$;
3: **end for**

4.3.3 The Third Algorithm

As mentioned in the last subsection, the second algorithm finds a proper local encoding kernel at the source node for the given local encoding kernels at all internal nodes with some constraints. In the following, from another perspective, another approach to construct network MDS codes will be studied, which designs proper local encoding kernels at all internal nodes for a given local encoding kernel at the source node s with some constraints.

We first give an informal description of the approach. The approach starts with a given local encoding kernel at the source node s with some minimum distance constraints. To be specific, this local encoding kernel K_s of size $\omega \times |Out(s)| = \omega \times n_s$ is regarded as a generator matrix of a linear code, but its minimum distance constraints are different from that in classical coding theory. Then an inductive method is used to design all the other local encoding kernels: begin with the simplest network that the source node and the sink nodes are connected with parallel channels, and then extend the network by one channel in each iteration until the network becomes the one we want; for each iteration, choose the proper local encoding coefficients for the new updated channel in order to preserve the minimum distances for all sinks.

Next, we will describe the approach formally. At the beginning, find C_t channel-disjoint paths from the source node s to each sink node $t \in T$. In this part, we assume that every channel in the network is on at least one of the $\sum_{t \in T} C_t$ paths we have found. Otherwise, delete those channels and the nodes that are not on any such path, and consider this new network. This is because a linear network error correction code for the new network can be extended to the original network without changing the minimum distances by assigning zero to all the local encoding coefficients associated with the deleted channels.

We consider an ancestral order on all channels which satisfy that it is consistent with the natural partial order on all channels and the first n_s channels are in $Out(s)$. Then given a network $G = (V, E)$, we construct a sequence of networks $G^i = (V^i, E^i)$, $i = 0, 1, 2, \cdots, |E| - n_s$ as follows. First, $G^0 = (V^0, E^0)$ is a subnetwork of G containing only n_s channels in $Out(s)$ with associated head nodes and all sink nodes. Following the order on E, in the ith iteration, $G^{i-1} = (V^{i-1}, E^{i-1})$ is expanded into $G^i = (V^i, E^i)$ by appending the next channel with the associated node in E. This procedure is repeated until G^i eventually becomes G. Note that G^i

contains $n_s + i$ channels and $G^{|E|-n_s} = G$. In each G^i, a sink node t has C_t incoming channels, where the jth incoming channel is the most downstream channel in the truncation in G^i of the jth channel-disjoint path from s to t in G. With a slight abuse of notation, still denote by $In(t)$ the set of incoming channels of a sink node $t \in T$ in G^i, when G^i is implied by the context. Figure 4.3 below illustrates G^0, G^1, G^2 and G^3 when G is the butterfly network as described in Fig. 1.2a.

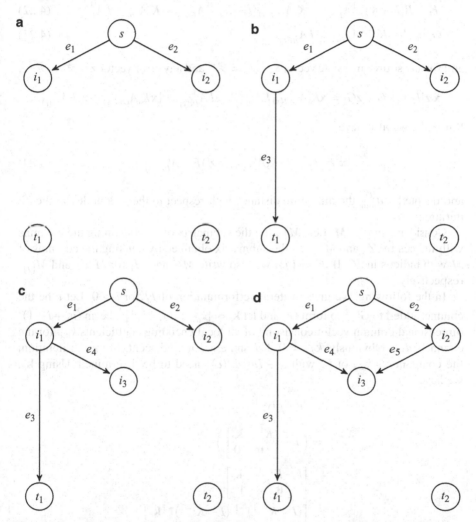

Fig. 4.3 Example of G_0, G_1, G_2 and G_3 for butterfly network G in Fig. 1.2a. Let the two channel-disjoint paths from s to t_1 and t_2 be $P_{t_1} = \{(e_1,e_3),\ (e_2,e_5,e_7,e_8)\}$ and $P_{t_2} = \{(e_1,e_4,e_7,e_9),\ (e_2,e_6)\}$, respectively. In G_0, $In(t_1) = In(t_2) = \{e_1,e_2\}$. In G_1, $In(t_1) = \{e_3,e_2\}$, $In(t_2) = \{e_1,e_2\}$. In G_2, $In(t_1) = \{e_3,e_2\}$, $In(t_2) = \{e_4,e_2\}$. In G_3, $In(t_1) = \{e_3,e_5\}$, $In(t_2) = \{e_4,e_2\}$. (**a**) G_0 for butterfly network, (**b**) G_1 for butterfly network, (**c**) G_2 for butterfly network, (**d**) G_3 for butterfly network

For the given proper local encoding kernel at the source node s, the approach constructs local encoding coefficients starting with G^0. For G^{i+1}, except for the new channel, all the local encoding coefficients in G^{i+1} are inherited from G^i. We define $K^i, F^i, F_t^i, G_t^i, \tilde{F}_t^i, F_{s,t}^i, A_\rho^i$ and $\mathbf{z}^i$ for the network G^i similar to $K, F, F_t, G_t, \tilde{F}_t, F_{s,t}, A_\rho$ and $\mathbf{z}$ defined for the original network G, respectively. Further, recall that for any sink node $t \in T$,

$$F_t = B(I - K)^{-1}A_{In(t)}^\top = K_s A_{Out(s)}(I - K)^{-1}A_{In(t)}^\top = K_s A_{Out(s)}FA_{In(t)}^\top, \quad (4.22)$$

$$G_t = (I - K)^{-1}A_{In(t)}^\top = FA_{In(t)}^\top, \quad (4.23)$$

and for any source message vector $\mathbf{x} \in \mathcal{X} = \mathcal{F}^\omega$ and any error vector $\mathbf{z} \in \mathcal{Z} = \mathcal{F}^{|E|}$,

$$[\mathbf{x}\,\mathbf{z}]\tilde{F}_t = \mathbf{x}F_t + \mathbf{z}G_t = \mathbf{x}K_s A_{Out(s)}FA_{In(t)}^\top + \mathbf{z}FA_{In(t)}^\top = (\mathbf{x}K_s A_{Out(s)} + \mathbf{z})FA_{In(t)}^\top.$$

Similarly, we also have

$$\left[\mathbf{x}\,\mathbf{z}^i\right]\tilde{F}_t^i = (\mathbf{x}K_s A_{Out(s)}^i + \mathbf{z}^i)F^i\left(A_{In(t)}^i\right)^\top, \quad (4.24)$$

and denote by $d_{\min}^{(t),i}$ the minimum distance with respect to the sink node t at the ith iteration.

Consider a matrix M. Let $(M)_{\mathcal{L}}$ be the submatrix of M containing the columns with indices in $\mathcal{L}$, and $M^{\backslash\mathcal{L}}$ be the submatrix obtained by deleting the columns of M with indices in $\mathcal{L}$. If $\mathcal{L} = \{j\}$, we also write $M^{\backslash j}$ and M_j for $M^{\backslash\{j\}}$ and $M_{\{j\}}$, respectively.

In the following, we give an iterative formulation of $\tilde{F}_t^i$ for $i > 0$. Let e be the channel added to G^{i-1} to form G^i, and let $\mathbf{k}_e = \begin{bmatrix} k_{d,e} : d \in E^{i-1} \end{bmatrix}^\top$ be an $(n_s + i - 1)$-dimensional column vector consisting of all local encoding coefficients $k_{d,e}$ for the channels d, e. Obviously, $k_{d,e} = 0$ if d and e are not adjacent. In the ith iteration, the components $k_{d,e}$ of $\mathbf{k}_e$ with $d \in In(tail(e))$ need to be determined. Using $\mathbf{k}_e$, we have

$$
\begin{aligned}
F^i &= (I - K^i)^{-1} \\
&= \left(I - \begin{bmatrix} K^{i-1} & \mathbf{k}_e \\ \mathbf{0} & 0 \end{bmatrix}\right)^{-1} \\
&= \begin{bmatrix} I - K^{i-1} & -\mathbf{k}_e \\ \mathbf{0} & 1 \end{bmatrix}^{-1} \\
&= \begin{bmatrix} (I - K^{i-1})^{-1} & (I - K^{i-1})^{-1}\mathbf{k}_e \\ \mathbf{0} & 1 \end{bmatrix} \\
&= \begin{bmatrix} F^{i-1} & F^{i-1}\mathbf{k}_e \\ \mathbf{0} & 1 \end{bmatrix}, \quad (4.25)
\end{aligned}
$$

where I represents the identity matrix but its size is determined depending on the context, both matrices F^i and K^i are of size $|E^i| \times |E^i| = (n_s + i) \times (n_s + i)$. Further, the $|Out(s)| \times |E^i| = n_s \times (n_s + i)$ matrix $A^i_{Out(s)}$ has one more zero column than $|Out(s)| \times |E^{i-1}| = n_s \times (n_s + i - 1)$ matrix $A^{i-1}_{Out(s)}$, i.e.,

$$A^i_{Out(s)} = \begin{bmatrix} A^{i-1}_{Out(s)} & \mathbf{0} \end{bmatrix}. \tag{4.26}$$

We consider the following two different cases.

Case 1. If the channel e is not on any chosen path from s to t, we only need to append a zero column to $A^{i-1}_{In(t)}$ to form $A^i_{In(t)}$, i.e.,

$$A^i_{In(t)} = \begin{bmatrix} A^{i-1}_{In(t)} & \mathbf{0} \end{bmatrix}, \tag{4.27}$$

where $A^i_{In(t)}$ and $A^{i-1}_{In(t)}$ are of sizes $|In(t)| \times |E^i| = C_t \times (n_s + i)$ and $|In(t)| \times |E^{i-1}| = C_t \times (n_s + i - 1)$, respectively. For this case, one obtains from (4.24)–(4.27)

$$
\begin{aligned}
\begin{bmatrix} \mathbf{x} & \mathbf{z}^i \end{bmatrix} \tilde{F}^i_t &= (\mathbf{x} K_s A^i_{Out(s)} + \mathbf{z}^i) F^i (A^i_{In(t)})^\top \\
&= (\mathbf{x} K_s A^i_{Out(s)} + \mathbf{z}^i) \begin{bmatrix} F^{i-1} & F^{i-1}\mathbf{k}_e \\ \mathbf{0} & 1 \end{bmatrix} \begin{bmatrix} \left(A^{i-1}_{In(t)} \right)^\top \\ \mathbf{0} \end{bmatrix} \\
&= (\mathbf{x} K_s A^i_{Out(s)} + \mathbf{z}^i) \begin{bmatrix} F^{i-1}(A^{i-1}_{In(t)})^\top \\ \mathbf{0} \end{bmatrix} \\
&= \left(\mathbf{x} K_s \begin{bmatrix} A^{i-1}_{Out(s)} & \mathbf{0} \end{bmatrix} + \begin{bmatrix} (\mathbf{z}^i)^{\backslash i} & (\mathbf{z}^i)_i \end{bmatrix} \right) \begin{bmatrix} F^{i-1}(A^{i-1}_{In(t)})^\top \\ \mathbf{0} \end{bmatrix} \\
&= \left(\mathbf{x} K_s A^{i-1}_{Out(s)} + (\mathbf{z}^i)^{\backslash i} \right) F^{i-1}(A^{i-1}_{In(t)})^\top \\
&= \mathbf{x} F^{i-1}_t + (\mathbf{z}^i)^{\backslash i} G^{i-1}_t \\
&= \begin{bmatrix} \mathbf{x} & (\mathbf{z}^i)^{\backslash i} \end{bmatrix} \tilde{F}^{i-1}_t. \tag{4.28}
\end{aligned}
$$

Note that $(\mathbf{z}^i)^{\backslash i}$ is an $(n_s + i - 1)$-dimensional error vector obtained by deleting the $(n_s + i)$th component of $\mathbf{z}^i$, which corresponds to e.

Case 2. Otherwise, if channel e is on the jth channel-disjoint path from the source node s to the sink node t, in order to form $A^i_{In(t)}$, besides appending a zero column with to $A^{i-1}_{In(t)}$, move the unique "1" in the jth row to the last component of that row. That is, if

$$
A^{i-1}_{In(t)} = \begin{bmatrix} \mathbf{b}_1 \\ \vdots \\ \mathbf{b}_{j-1} \\ \mathbf{b}_j \\ \mathbf{b}_{j+1} \\ \mathbf{b}_{C_t} \end{bmatrix}, \text{ then } A^i_{In(t)} = \begin{bmatrix} \mathbf{b}_1 & 0 \\ \vdots & \vdots \\ \mathbf{b}_{j-1} & 0 \\ \mathbf{0} & 1 \\ \mathbf{b}_{j+1} & 0 \\ \vdots & \vdots \\ \mathbf{b}_{C_t} & 0 \end{bmatrix}. \tag{4.29}
$$

Subsequently, one has from (4.24), (4.25), (4.26) and (4.29)

$$
\begin{aligned}
\left([\mathbf{x}\ \mathbf{z}^i]\ \tilde{F}_t^i \right)_j &= \left[(\mathbf{x}K_s A_{Out(s)}^i + \mathbf{z}^i) F^i (A_{In(t)}^i)^\top \right]_j \\
&= (\mathbf{x}K_s A_{Out(s)}^i + \mathbf{z}^i) \begin{bmatrix} F^{i-1} & F^{i-1}\mathbf{k}_e \\ 0 & 1 \end{bmatrix} \left((A_{In(t)}^i)^\top \right)_j \\
&= (\mathbf{x}K_s A_{Out(s)}^i + \mathbf{z}^i) \begin{bmatrix} F^{i-1} & F^{i-1}\mathbf{k}_e \\ 0 & 1 \end{bmatrix} \begin{bmatrix} 0 \\ 1 \end{bmatrix} \\
&= (\mathbf{x}K_s A_{Out(s)}^i + \mathbf{z}^i) \begin{bmatrix} F^{i-1}\mathbf{k}_e \\ 1 \end{bmatrix} \\
&= \left(\mathbf{x}K_s \begin{bmatrix} A_{Out(s)}^{i-1} & 0 \end{bmatrix} + [(\mathbf{z}^i)^{\backslash i}\ (\mathbf{z}^i)_i] \right) \begin{bmatrix} F^{i-1}\mathbf{k}_e \\ 1 \end{bmatrix} \\
&= \left(\mathbf{x}K_s A_{Out(s)}^{i-1} + (\mathbf{z}^i)^{\backslash i} \right) F^{i-1}\mathbf{k}_e + (\mathbf{z}^i)_i, \qquad\qquad (4.30)
\end{aligned}
$$

and

$$
\begin{aligned}
\left([\mathbf{x}\ \mathbf{z}^i]\ \tilde{F}_t^i \right)^{\backslash j} &= (\mathbf{x}K_s A_{Out(s)}^i + \mathbf{z}^i) F^i \left((A_{In(t)}^i)^\top \right)^{\backslash j} \\
&= (\mathbf{x}K_s A_{Out(s)}^i + \mathbf{z}^i) \begin{bmatrix} F^{i-1} & F^{i-1}\mathbf{k}_e \\ 0 & 1 \end{bmatrix} \begin{bmatrix} \mathbf{b}_1^\top & \cdots & \mathbf{b}_{j-1}^\top & \mathbf{b}_{j+1}^\top & \cdots & \mathbf{b}_{C_t}^\top \\ 0 & \cdots & 0 & 0 & \cdots & 0 \end{bmatrix} \\
&= (\mathbf{x}K_s A_{Out(s)}^i + \mathbf{z}^i) \begin{bmatrix} F^{i-1}\mathbf{b}_1^\top & \cdots & F^{i-1}\mathbf{b}_{j-1}^\top & F^{i-1}\mathbf{b}_{j+1}^\top & \cdots & F^{i-1}\mathbf{b}_{C_t}^\top \\ 0 & \cdots & 0 & 0 & \cdots & 0 \end{bmatrix} \\
&= (\mathbf{x}K_s A_{Out(s)}^i + \mathbf{z}^i) \begin{bmatrix} F^{i-1} \left[(A_{In(t)}^{i-1})^\top \right]^{\backslash j} \\ 0 \end{bmatrix} \\
&= \left(\mathbf{x}K_s \begin{bmatrix} A_{Out(s)}^{i-1} & 0 \end{bmatrix} + [(\mathbf{z}^i)^{\backslash i}\ (\mathbf{z}^i)_i] \right) \begin{bmatrix} F^{i-1} \left[(A_{In(t)}^{i-1})^\top \right]^{\backslash j} \\ 0 \end{bmatrix} \\
&= (\mathbf{x}K_s A_{Out(s)}^{i-1} + (\mathbf{z}^i)^{\backslash i}) F^{i-1} \left[(A_{In(t)}^{i-1})^\top \right]^{\backslash j} \\
&= \left[(\mathbf{x}K_s A_{Out(s)}^{i-1} + (\mathbf{z}^i)^{\backslash i}) F^{i-1} (A_{In(t)}^{i-1})^\top \right]^{\backslash j} \\
&= \left[[\mathbf{x}\ (\mathbf{z}^i)^{\backslash i}]\ \tilde{F}_t^{i-1} \right]^{\backslash j}. \qquad\qquad (4.31)
\end{aligned}
$$

After the above preparation, we begin to describe the algorithm in detail. First, construct the local encoding kernel K_s at the source node s satisfying $d_{\min}^{(t),0} = C_t - \omega + 1$ for each sink node $t \in T$. To be specific, note that for $i = 0$, $A_{Out(s)}^0$ is an $n_s \times n_s$ identity matrix and K^0 is an $n_s \times n_s$ zero matrix. So $F^0 = (I - K^0)^{-1} = I$ is an $n_s \times n_s$ identity matrix. Thus, from (4.22)

$$
F_t^0 = K_s A_{Out(s)}^0 F^0 (A_{In(t)}^0)^\top = K_s (A_{In(t)}^0)^\top \triangleq (K_s)_{In(t)},
$$

which consists of $|In(t)| = C_t$ column vectors indexed by the C_t paths from s to t. And from (4.23),

$$G_t^0 = F^0(A_{In(t)}^0)^\top = (A_{In(t)}^0)^\top,$$

which implies that $\mathbf{z}^0 G_t^0 = \mathbf{z}_{In(t)}^0$. Hence,

$$d^{(t)}(\mathbf{x}_1 F_t^0, \mathbf{x}_2 F_t^0) = \min\{w_H(\mathbf{z}^0) : \mathbf{z}^0 \in \mathscr{F}^{n_s} \text{ such that } (\mathbf{x}_1 - \mathbf{x}_2)(K_s)_{In(t)} = \mathbf{z}_{In(t)}^0\}$$
$$= w_H\left((\mathbf{x}_1 - \mathbf{x}_2)(K_s)_{In(t)}\right).$$

This implies that

$$d_{\min}^{(t),0} = \min\{w_H\left((\mathbf{x}_1 - \mathbf{x}_2)(K_s)_{In(t)}\right) : \text{ all distinct } \mathbf{x}_1, \mathbf{x}_2 \in \mathscr{F}^\omega\}$$
$$= \min_{0 \neq \mathbf{x} \in \mathscr{F}^\omega} w_H\left(\mathbf{x} \cdot (K_s)_{In(t)}\right).$$

Thus, if we regard $(K_s)_{In(t)}$ as an $\omega \times C_t$ generator matrix of a linear code, then $d_{\min}^{(t),0}$ is the minimum Hamming weight of this linear code of generator matrix $(K_s)_{In(t)}$. Therefore, $d_{\min}^{(t),0} = C_t - \omega + 1$ for all sink nodes $t \in T$ mean that the minimum Hamming weight of the corresponding linear code of generator matrix $(K_s)_{In(t)}$ is equal to $C_t - \omega + 1$ for all sinks $t \in T$.

Assume that the local encoding kernel K_s at the source node s satisfying constraints $d_{\min}^{(t),0} = C_t - \omega + 1$ for each sink node $t \in T$ is given. The following is the procedure to choose $\mathbf{k}_e$ for each channel $e \in E \backslash Out(s)$ as the given upstream-to-downstream order. Let e be the channel appended to the network in the ith step. Then we choose $\mathbf{k}_e$ such that the following "*feasible condition*" is satisfied:

$$\left([\mathbf{x} \ -\mathbf{z}^i] \tilde{F}_t^i\right)^{\backslash \mathscr{L}} = \left(\mathbf{x} F_t^i - \mathbf{z}^i G_t^i\right)^{\backslash \mathscr{L}} \neq \mathbf{0},$$

or equivalently,

$$\left((\mathbf{x} K_s A_{Out(s)}^i - \mathbf{z}^i) F^i (A_{In(t)}^i)^\top\right)^{\backslash \mathscr{L}} \neq \mathbf{0},$$

for all combinations of

(C1) $t \in T$;
(C2) $\mathscr{L} \subset \{1, 2, \cdots, C_t\}$ with $0 \leq |\mathscr{L}| \leq C_t - \omega$;
(C3) nonzero message vector $\mathbf{x} \in \mathscr{F}^\omega$;
(C4) error vector $\mathbf{z}^i \in \mathscr{F}^{n_s + i}$ with $w_H(\mathbf{z}^i) \leq C_t - \omega - |\mathscr{L}|$.

Note that this feasible condition is required for each iteration. As we will show, the feasible condition is sufficient for $d_{\min}^{(t),i} \geq C_t - \omega + 1, t \in T$, which, together with the Singleton bound $d_{\min}^{(t),i} \leq C_t - \omega + 1$, is sufficient for $d_{\min}^{(t),i} = C_t - \omega + 1$. Thus, when the procedure terminates, the linear network error correction code constructed for G satisfies $d_{\min}^{(t)} = C_t - \omega + 1$ for all $t \in T$, which is MDS.

In the following, we will indicate that the feasible condition in ith iteration implies $d_{\min}^{(t),i} = C_t - \omega + 1$ for all $t \in T$. Assume the contrary that $d_{\min}^{(t),i} < C_t - \omega + 1$, or $d_{\min}^{(t),i} \leq C_t - \omega$ for some $t \in T$, although the feasible condition is satisfied. Let $\mathbf{x}_1, \mathbf{x}_2$ be two distinct message vectors in $\mathscr{F}^\omega$ such that

$$d^{(t),i}(\mathbf{x}_1 F_t^i, \mathbf{x}_2 F_t^i) = d_{\min}^{(t),i} \leq C_t - \omega.$$

Since

$$d^{(t),i}(\mathbf{x}_1 F_t^i, \mathbf{x}_2 F_t^i) = \min\{w_H(\mathbf{z}^i) : \mathbf{z}^i \in \mathscr{F}^{n_s+i} \text{ such that } (\mathbf{x}_1 - \mathbf{x}_2)F_t^i = \mathbf{z}^i G_t^i\},$$

without loss of generality, let $\mathbf{z}^i$ be an error vector in $\mathscr{F}^{n_s+i}$ with $w_H(\mathbf{z}^i) = d_{\min}^{(t),i}$ such that $(\mathbf{x}_1 - \mathbf{x}_2)F_t^i = \mathbf{z}^i G_t^i$, that is, there exists a nonzero vector $\mathbf{x}_1 - \mathbf{x}_2$ in $\mathscr{F}^\omega$ and an error vector $\mathbf{z}^i$ in $\mathscr{F}^{n_s+i}$ with $w_H(\mathbf{z}^i) = d_{\min}^{(t),i} \leq C_t - \omega$ such that

$$(\mathbf{x}_1 - \mathbf{x}_2)F_t^i - \mathbf{z}^i G_t^i = \begin{bmatrix} \mathbf{x}_1 - \mathbf{x}_2 & \mathbf{z}^i \end{bmatrix} \tilde{F}_t^i = \mathbf{0}.$$

This is a contradiction to the feasible condition with $\mathscr{L} = \emptyset$.

The above procedure is described in the following Algorithm 4. Furthermore, the following result shows that the feasible condition can be always satisfied when the field size is sufficiently large.

Theorem 4.8. *Given a local encoding kernel K_s at the source node s with $d_{\min}^{(t),0} = C_t - \omega + 1$ for all sink nodes $t \in T$, there exist local encoding coefficients such that the feasible condition is satisfied for $i = 1, 2, \cdots, |E| - n_s$ when the field size is larger than $\sum_{t \in T} \binom{C_t + |E| - 2}{C_t - \omega}$.*

Moreover, by Yang et al. [50], the time complexity of Algorithm 4 is:

$$\mathcal{O}\left(\gamma |E| \sum_{t \in T} \binom{|E| + C_t - 2}{\delta_t} \left[\gamma^2 + \sum_{t \in T} \binom{|E| + C_t - 2}{\delta_t} \right] \right),$$

where γ is the maximum incoming degree of each node in G.

Algorithm 4 Construct local encoding coefficients to obtain linear network error correction MDS codes

Input: The single source multicast network $G = (V, E)$, the information rate $\omega \leq \min_{t \in T} C_t$, and the local encoding kernel K_s at the source node s such that $d_{\min}^{(t),0} = C_t - \omega + 1$ for each sink node $t \in T$.

Output: The local encoding kernels for all internal nodes in G such that the linear network error correction code is MDS.

1: **for each** $t \in T$ **do**
2:     choose C_t channel-disjoint paths from s to t;
3: **end for**
4: Initialize $F = I$, $A_{Out(s)} = I$;
5: **for each** $e \in E \backslash Out(s)$ in an upstream-to-downstream order **do**
6:     $\Gamma = \emptyset$;
7:     **for each** $t \in T$ **do**
8:         **if** no chosen path from s to t crosses e **then**
9:             $A_{In(t)} = \begin{bmatrix} A_{In(t)} & \mathbf{0} \end{bmatrix}$;
10:         **else if** e is on the jth path from s to t **then**
11:             **for each** $\mathscr{L}$ with $|\mathscr{L}| \leq C_t - \omega$ and $j \notin \mathscr{L}$ **do**
12:                 **for each** ρ with $|\rho| = C_t - \omega - |\mathscr{L}|$ **do**
13:                     Find $\mathbf{x}_0 \neq \mathbf{0}$ and $\mathbf{z}_0$ matching ρ such that

$$\left(\begin{bmatrix} \mathbf{x}_0 & -\mathbf{z}_0 \end{bmatrix} \tilde{F}_t \right)^{\backslash \mathscr{L} \cup \{j\}} = \mathbf{0};$$

14:                     **if** exist $\mathbf{x}_0$ and $\mathbf{z}_0$ **then**
15:                         $\Gamma = \Gamma \cup \{\mathbf{k} : (\mathbf{x}_0 K_s A_{Out(s)} - \mathbf{z}_0) F \mathbf{k} = \mathbf{0}\}$;
16:                     **end if**
17:                 **end for**
18:             **end for**
19:         **end if**
20:         update $A_{In(t)}$ using (4.29);
21:     **end for**
22:     choose $\mathbf{k}_e$ in $\mathscr{F}^{|In(tail(e))|} \backslash \Gamma$;
23:     $F = \begin{bmatrix} F & F\mathbf{k}_e \\ \mathbf{0} & 1 \end{bmatrix}$;
24: **end for**

Chapter 5
Random Linear Network Error Correction Coding

As discussed in Chap. 1, random linear network coding is feasible for noncoherent networks without errors, and its performance analysis is very important in theory and applications. This random method also can be applied to network error correction. Similarly, each node (maybe the source node s) randomly and uniformly picks the local encoding coefficients from the base field $\mathscr{F}$ for each outgoing channel, which are used to construct extended global encoding kernels and encode the received messages. That is, these local coding coefficients $k_{d,e}$ for linear network error correction coding are still independently and uniformly distributed random variables taking values in the base field $\mathscr{F}$. Further, the linear network error correction codes constructed by this method are called *random linear network error correction codes*. For this random linear network error correction coding, we have to consider two aspects, information transmission and error correction, in order to analyze its performance. In this chapter, we will investigate the performance of random linear network error correction codes. At first, random LNEC MDS codes are under consideration. Before the discussion, we give the following definitions.

Definition 5.1. Let G be a single source multicast network, $\mathbf{C}$ be a random linear network error correction code on G, and $d_{\min}^{(t)}$ be the minimum distance at a sink node t of $\mathbf{C}$.

- $P_{ec}(t) \triangleq Pr(\{\dim(\Phi(t)) < \omega\} \cup \{d_{\min}^{(t)} < \delta_t + 1\})$ is called the failure probability of random linear network error correction MDS coding for sink node t.
- $P_{ec} \triangleq Pr(\{\mathbf{C} \text{ is not regular}\} \cup \{\exists\ t \in T \text{ such that } d_{\min}^{(t)} < \delta_t + 1\})$ is called the failure probability of random linear network error correction MDS coding for the network G, that is, the probability that network MDS codes are not constructed by the random method.

In order to evaluate these two failure probabilities, the following lemma is useful.

X. Guang and Z. Zhang, *Linear Network Error Correction Coding*, SpringerBriefs in Computer Science, DOI 10.1007/978-1-4939-0588-1_5, © The Author(s) 2014

Lemma 5.1. *Let $\mathscr{L}$ be an n dimensional linear space over a finite field $\mathscr{F}$, $\mathscr{L}_0$, $\mathscr{L}_1$ be two subspaces of $\mathscr{L}$ of dimensions k_0, k_1, respectively, and $\langle\mathscr{L}_0\cup\mathscr{L}_1\rangle = \mathscr{L}$. Let $l_1, l_2, \cdots, l_m$ $(m = n - k_0)$ be m independently and uniformly distributed random vectors taking values in $\mathscr{L}_1$. Then*

$$Pr(\dim(\langle\mathscr{L}_0\cup\{l_1, l_2, \cdots, l_m\}\rangle) = n) = \prod_{i=1}^{m}\left(1 - \frac{1}{|\mathscr{F}|^i}\right).$$

Proof. First, define a sequence of subspaces of $\mathscr{L}$:

$$O_0 = \mathscr{L}_0\cap\mathscr{L}_1,$$
$$O_1 = \langle O_0\cup\{l_1\}\rangle,$$
$$O_2 = \langle O_1\cup\{l_2\}\rangle = \langle O_0\cup\{l_1,l_2\}\rangle,$$
$$\cdots$$
$$O_m = \langle O_{m-1}\cup\{l_m\}\rangle = \langle O_0\cup\{l_1,l_2,\cdots,l_m\}\rangle.$$

Since $\dim(\langle\mathscr{L}_0\cup\mathscr{L}_1\rangle) = n$ and $\dim(\mathscr{L}_i) = k_i$ $(i = 0, 1)$, it follows that

$$\dim(O_0) = \dim(\mathscr{L}_0) + \dim(\mathscr{L}_1) - \dim(\langle\mathscr{L}_0\cup\mathscr{L}_1\rangle) = k_0 + k_1 - n.$$

And note that the event "$\dim(\langle\mathscr{L}_0\cup\{l_1, l_2, \cdots, l_m\}\rangle) = n$" is equivalent to the event "$l_1 \notin O_0, l_2 \notin O_1, \cdots, l_m \notin O_{m-1}$", which implies that

$$Pr(\dim(\langle\mathscr{L}_0\cup\{l_1,l_2,\cdots,l_m\}\rangle) = n)$$
$$= Pr(l_1 \notin O_0, l_2 \notin O_1, \cdots, l_m \notin O_{m-1})$$
$$= Pr(l_m \notin O_{m-1}|l_{m-1} \notin O_{m-2}, \cdots, l_1 \notin O_0)$$
$$\cdot Pr(l_{m-1} \notin O_{m-2}|l_{m-2} \notin O_{m-3}, \cdots, l_1 \notin O_0)$$
$$\cdots Pr(l_2 \notin O_1|l_1 \notin O_0)\cdot Pr(l_1 \notin O_0)$$
$$= \prod_{i=0}^{m-1}\left(1 - \frac{|\mathscr{F}|^{\dim(O_0)+i}}{|\mathscr{F}|^{k_1}}\right)$$
$$= \prod_{i=0}^{m-1}\left(1 - \frac{1}{|\mathscr{F}|^{m-i}}\right)$$
$$= \prod_{i=1}^{m}\left(1 - \frac{1}{|\mathscr{F}|^i}\right)$$
$$= \prod_{i=1}^{n-k_0}\left(1 - \frac{1}{|\mathscr{F}|^i}\right).$$

This completes the proof.   □

Motivated by Algorithm 2 for constructing LNEC codes, an analysis approach can be obtained to analyze the performance of random LNEC coding, which derives the following results.

Theorem 5.1. *Let G be a single source multicast network, and the information rate* $\omega \leq \min_{t \in T} C_t$. *Using random method to construct a linear network error correction MDS code, then*

- *for each* $t \in T$, *the failure probability of random linear network error correction MDS coding for t satisfies:*

$$P_{ec}(t) < 1 - \left(1 - \frac{|R_t(\delta_t)|}{|\mathscr{F}| - 1}\right)^{|J|+1};$$

- *the failure probability of random linear network error correction MDS coding for the network G satisfies:*

$$P_{ec} < 1 - \left(1 - \frac{\sum_{t \in T} |R_t(\delta_t)|}{|\mathscr{F}| - 1}\right)^{|J|+1},$$

where J is the set of internal nodes in G.

Proof. For the single source multicast network $G = (V, E)$, s is the single source node, T is the set of the sink nodes, $J = V - \{s\} - T$ is the set of the internal nodes, and E is the set of all channels. Let $\tilde{G} = (\tilde{V}, \tilde{E})$ be the extended network of G.

For each sink node $t \in T$ and each error pattern $\rho \in R_t(\delta_t)$, Corollary 4.2 implies that there are $(\omega + \delta_t)$ channel-disjoint paths from either $In(s)$ or ρ' to t satisfying the properties that (1) there exist exactly δ_t channel-disjoint paths from ρ' to t, and ω channel-disjoint paths from $In(s)$ to t; (2) each of these δ_t paths from ρ' to t starts with a channel $e' \in \rho'$ and passes through the corresponding channel $e \in \rho$. Denote by $\mathscr{P}_{t,\rho}$ the set of $(\omega + \delta_t)$ channel-disjoint paths satisfying these properties and by $E_{t,\rho}$ the set of all channels in $\mathscr{P}_{t,\rho}$.

Note that the event "$\{\dim(\Phi(t)) = \omega\} \cap \{d_{\min}^{(t)} = \delta_t + 1\}$" is equivalent to the event "$\{\dim(\Phi(t)) = \omega\} \cap \{\forall \rho \in R_t(\delta_t) : \Phi(t) \cap \Delta(t, \rho) = \{0\}\}$", and furthermore, the event "$\forall \rho \in R_t(\delta_t) : \text{Rank}(\tilde{F}_t^\rho) = \omega + \delta_t$" implies the event "$\{\dim(\Phi(t)) = \omega\} \cap \{\forall \rho \in R_t(\delta_t) : \Phi(t) \cap \Delta(t, \rho) = \{0\}\}$". Thus, it suffices to consider the following probability:

$$Pr(\cap_{\rho \in R_t(\delta_t)} \text{Rank}(\tilde{F}_t^\rho) = \omega + \delta_t).$$

For the network G, let an ancestral order of nodes be

$$s \prec i_1 \prec i_2 \prec \cdots \prec i_{|J|} \prec T.$$

During our discussion, we use the concept of cuts of the paths similar to the dynamic set $CUT_{t,\rho}$ as mentioned in Algorithm 2. The first cut is $CUT_{t,\rho,0} = In(s) \cup \{e' : e \in \rho\}$, i.e., the ω imaginary message channels $d_1', d_2', \cdots, d_\omega'$ and imaginary error channels corresponding to those in ρ. At the source node s, the next $CUT_{t,\rho,1}$ is formed from $CUT_{t,\rho,0}$ by replacing those channels in $\{In(s) \cup \{e' : e \in Out(s)\}\} \cap CUT_{t,\rho,0}$ by their respective next channels in the paths. These new channels are in $Out(s) \cap E_{t,\rho}$. Other channels remain the same as in $CUT_{t,\rho,0}$. At node i_1, the next cut $CUT_{t,\rho,2}$ is formed from $CUT_{t,\rho,1}$ by replacing those channels in

$\{In(i_1) \cup \{e' : e \in Out(i_1)\}\} \cap CUT_{t,\rho,1}$ by their respective next channels in the paths. These new channels are in $Out(i_1) \cap E_{t,\rho}$. Other channels remain the same as in $CUT_{t,\rho,1}$. Subsequently, once $CUT_{t,\rho,k}$ is defined, $CUT_{t,\rho,k+1}$ is formed from $CUT_{t,\rho,k}$ by the same method. By induction, all cuts $CUT_{t,\rho,k}$ for $t \in T$, $\rho \in R_t(\delta_t)$, and $k = 0, 1, 2, \cdots, |J| + 1$ can be defined. Moreover, for each $CUT_{t,\rho,k}$, we divide $CUT_{t,\rho,k}$ into two disjoint parts $CUT_{t,\rho,k}^{in}$ and $CUT_{t,\rho,k}^{out}$ as follows:

$$CUT_{t,\rho,k}^{in} = \{e : e \in CUT_{t,\rho,k} \cap In(i_k)\},$$
$$CUT_{t,\rho,k}^{out} = \{e : e \in CUT_{t,\rho,k} \setminus CUT_{t,\rho,k}^{in}\}.$$

Define $(\omega + \delta_t) \times (\omega + \delta_t)$ matrices $\tilde{F}_t^{\rho(k)} = \left[\tilde{f}_e^{\rho} : e \in CUT_{t,\rho,k} \right]$, $k = 0, 1, \cdots, |J| + 1$. If $\text{Rank}(\tilde{F}_t^{\rho(k)}) < \omega + \delta_t$, we say that we have a failure at $CUT_{t,\rho,k}$. Let $\Gamma_k^{(t,\rho)}$ represent the event "$\text{Rank}(\tilde{F}_t^{\rho(k)}) = \omega + \delta_t$". Furthermore, let $|J| = m$, and note that $\tilde{F}_t^{\rho(m+1)}$ is a submatrix of $\tilde{F}_t^{\rho}$. It follows that the event "$\forall \rho \in R_t(\delta_t)$, $\text{Rank}(\tilde{F}_t^{\rho(m+1)}) = \omega + \delta_t$" implies the event "$\forall \rho \in R_t(\delta_t), \text{Rank}(\tilde{F}_t^{\rho}) = \omega + \delta_t$". Therefore,

$$1 - P_{ec}(t)$$
$$= Pr(\{\dim(\Phi(t)) = \omega\} \cap \{d_{\min}^{(t)} = \delta_t + 1\})$$
$$= Pr(\{\dim(\Phi(t)) = \omega\} \cap \{\cap_{\rho \in R_t(\delta_t)} \Phi(t) \cap \Delta(t, \rho) = \{0\}\})$$
$$\geq Pr(\cap_{\rho \in R_t(\delta_t)} \text{Rank}(\tilde{F}_t^{\rho}) = \omega + \delta_t)$$
$$\geq Pr(\cap_{\rho \in R_t(\delta_t)} \Gamma_{m+1}^{(t,\rho)}).$$

Consequently,

$$Pr(\cap_{\rho \in R_t(\delta_t)} \Gamma_{m+1}^{(t,\rho)})$$
$$\geq Pr(\cap_{\rho \in R_t(\delta_t)} \Gamma_{m+1}^{(t,\rho)}, \cap_{\rho \in R_t(\delta_t)} \Gamma_m^{(t,\rho)}, \cdots, \cap_{\rho \in R_t(\delta_t)} \Gamma_0^{(t,\rho)})$$
$$\geq Pr(\cap_{\rho \in R_t(\delta_t)} \Gamma_{m+1}^{(t,\rho)} | \cap_{\rho \in R_t(\delta_t)} \Gamma_m^{(t,\rho)}) \qquad (5.1)$$
$$\cdots Pr(\cap_{\rho \in R_t(\delta_t)} \Gamma_1^{(t,\rho)} | \cap_{\rho \in R_t(\delta_t)} \Gamma_0^{(t,\rho)}) Pr(\cap_{\rho \in R_t(\delta_t)} \Gamma_0^{(t,\rho)})$$
$$= \prod_{k=0}^{m} Pr(\cap_{\rho \in R_t(\delta_t)} \Gamma_{k+1}^{(t,\rho)} | \cap_{\rho \in R_t(\delta_t)} \Gamma_k^{(t,\rho)}), \qquad (5.2)$$

where (5.2) follows from

$$Pr(\cap_{\rho \in R_t(\delta_t)} \Gamma_0^{(t,\rho)}) = Pr(\cap_{\rho \in R_t(\delta_t)} \text{Rank}([\tilde{f}_e^{\rho} : e \in In(s) \cup \rho']) = \omega + \delta_t)$$
$$= Pr(\text{Rank}(I_{\omega + \delta_t}) = \omega + \delta_t)$$
$$\equiv 1.$$

For each channel $e \in E$, let $e \in Out(i_k)$. Let $\tilde{g}_e$ be an independently and uniformly distributed random vector taking values in $\mathcal{L}(In(i_k)) = \langle\{\tilde{f}_d : d \in In(i_k)\}\rangle$. In other words, if $In(i_k) = \{d_1, d_2, \cdots, d_l\}$, then

$$\tilde{g}_e = k_{d_1,e} \tilde{f}_{d_1} + k_{d_2,e} \tilde{f}_{d_2} + \cdots + k_{d_l,e} \tilde{f}_{d_l},$$

where $k_{d_j,e}$, $j = 1, 2, \cdots, l$ are independently and uniformly distributed random variables taking values in the base field $\mathscr{F}$. It follows that

$$\tilde{g}_e^\rho = k_{d_1,e}\tilde{f}_{d_1}^\rho + k_{d_2,e}\tilde{f}_{d_2}^\rho + \cdots + k_{d_l,e}\tilde{f}_{d_l}^\rho$$

is also an independently and uniformly distributed random vector taking values in $\mathscr{L}^\rho(In(i_k)) = \langle\{\tilde{f}_d^\rho : d \in In(i_k)\}\rangle$. We always define $\tilde{f}_e = \tilde{g}_e + 1_e$ to preserve $\tilde{f}_e(e) = 1$. Therefore, for all $e \in E_{t,\rho} \cap Out(i_k)$ with $e(t,\rho) \in CUT_{t,\rho,k}^{in}$, i.e., $e \notin \rho$, it is shown that $\tilde{f}_e^\rho = \tilde{g}_e^\rho$ because of $e \notin \rho$. Thus, $\tilde{f}_e^\rho$ is an independently and uniformly distributed random vector taking values in $\mathscr{L}^\rho(In(i_k))$. Otherwise $e \in E_{t,\rho} \cap Out(i_k)$ with $e(t,\rho) \in CUT_{t,\rho,k}^{out}$, i.e., $e \in \rho$, or equivalently, $e(t,\rho) = e'$, then, $\tilde{f}_e^\rho$ and $\{\tilde{f}_d^\rho : d \in CUT_{t,\rho,k}\backslash e(t,\rho)\}$ are always linearly independent, since $\tilde{f}_e^\rho(e) = 1$ and $\tilde{f}_d^\rho(e) = 0$ for all $d \in CUT_{t,\rho,k}\backslash e(t,\rho)$.

Applying Lemma 5.1, we derive

$$\begin{aligned}
Pr(\Gamma_{k+1}^{(t,\rho)}|\Gamma_k^{(t,\rho)}) &= \prod_{i=1}^{|CUT_{t,\rho,k}^{in}|}\left(1 - \frac{1}{|\mathscr{F}|^i}\right) \\
&\geq \prod_{i=1}^{\omega+\delta_t}\left(1 - \frac{1}{|\mathscr{F}|^i}\right) \\
&> 1 - \sum_{i=1}^{\omega+\delta_t}\frac{1}{|\mathscr{F}|^i} \\
&> 1 - \sum_{i=1}^{\infty}\frac{1}{|\mathscr{F}|^i} \\
&= 1 - \frac{1}{|\mathscr{F}|-1}.
\end{aligned}$$

Consequently, for each k $(0 \leq k \leq m)$, one has

$$\begin{aligned}
&Pr(\cap_{\rho \in R_t(\delta_t)}\Gamma_{k+1}^{(t,\rho)}|\cap_{\rho \in R_t(\delta_t)}\Gamma_k^{(t,\rho)}) \\
&= 1 - Pr(\cup_{\rho \in R_t(\delta_t)}\Gamma_{k+1}^{(t,\rho)^c}|\cap_{\rho \in R_t(\delta_t)}\Gamma_k^{(t,\rho)}) \\
&\geq 1 - \sum_{\rho \in R_t(\delta_t)}Pr(\Gamma_{k+1}^{(t,\rho)^c}|\cap_{\rho \in R_t(\delta_t)}\Gamma_k^{(t,\rho)}) \\
&= 1 - \sum_{\rho \in R_t(\delta_t)}Pr(\Gamma_{k+1}^{(t,\rho)^c}|\Gamma_k^{(t,\rho)}) \\
&> 1 - \sum_{\rho \in R_t(\delta_t)}\frac{1}{|\mathscr{F}|-1} \\
&= 1 - \frac{|R_t(\delta_t)|}{|\mathscr{F}|-1}.
\end{aligned}$$

Combining the above inequalities, we have

$$1 - P_{ec}(t) \geq \prod_{k=0}^{m} Pr(\cap_{\rho \in R_t(\delta_t)} \Gamma_{k+1}^{(t,\rho)} | \cap_{\rho \in R_t(\delta_t)} \Gamma_k^{(t,\rho)}) > \left(1 - \frac{|R_t(\delta_t)|}{|\mathscr{F}| - 1} \right)^{m+1} .$$

That is,

$$P_{ec}(t) < 1 - \left(1 - \frac{|R_t(\delta_t)|}{|\mathscr{F}| - 1} \right)^{m+1} .$$

Next, we further consider P_{ec},

$$
\begin{aligned}
1 - P_{ec} &\geq Pr(\cap_{t \in T} \cap_{\rho \in R_t(\delta_t)} Rank(\tilde{F}_t^{\rho}) = \omega + \delta_t) \\
&\geq Pr(\cap_{t \in T} \cap_{\rho \in R_t(\delta_t)} \Gamma_{m+1}^{(t,\rho)}, \cap_{t \in T} \cap_{\rho \in R_t(\delta_t)} \Gamma_m^{(t,\rho)}, \cdots, \cap_{t \in T} \cap_{\rho \in R_t(\delta_t)} \Gamma_0^{(t,\rho)}) \\
&\geq Pr(\cap_{t \in T} \cap_{\rho \in R_t(\delta_t)} \Gamma_{m+1}^{(t,\rho)} | \cap_{t \in T} \cap_{\rho \in R_t(\delta_t)} \Gamma_m^{(t,\rho)}) \\
&\quad \cdot Pr(\cap_{t \in T} \cap_{\rho \in R_t(\delta_t)} \Gamma_m^{(t,\rho)} | \cap_{t \in T} \cap_{\rho \in R_t(\delta_t)} \Gamma_{m-1}^{(t,\rho)}) \\
&\quad \cdots \cdot Pr(\cap_{t \in T} \cap_{\rho \in R_t(\delta_t)} \Gamma_1^{(t,\rho)} | \cap_{t \in T} \cap_{\rho \in R_t(\delta_t)} \Gamma_0^{(t,\rho)}) \quad (5.3) \\
&= \prod_{k=0}^{m} Pr(\cap_{t \in T} \cap_{\rho \in R_t(\delta_t)} \Gamma_{k+1}^{(t,\rho)} | \cap_{t \in T} \cap_{\rho \in R_t(\delta_t)} \Gamma_k^{(t,\rho)}),
\end{aligned}
$$

where (5.3) follows from $Pr(\cap_{t \in T} \cap_{\rho \in R_t(\delta_t)} \Gamma_0^{(t,\rho)}) \equiv 1$.
Furthermore, for each k $(0 \leq k \leq m)$,

$$
\begin{aligned}
&Pr(\cap_{t \in T} \cap_{\rho \in R_t(\delta_t)} \Gamma_{k+1}^{(t,\rho)} | \cap_{t \in T} \cap_{\rho \in R_t(\delta_t)} \Gamma_k^{(t,\rho)}) \\
&= 1 - Pr(\cup_{t \in T} \cup_{\rho \in R_t(\delta_t)} \Gamma_{k+1}^{(t,\rho)^c} | \cap_{t \in T} \cap_{\rho \in R_t(\delta_t)} \Gamma_k^{(t,\rho)}) \\
&\geq 1 - \sum_{t \in T} \sum_{\rho \in R_t(\delta_t)} Pr(\Gamma_{k+1}^{(t,\rho)^c} | \Gamma_k^{(t,\rho)}) \\
&= 1 - \sum_{t \in T} \sum_{\rho \in R_t(\delta_t)} [1 - Pr(\Gamma_{k+1}^{(t,\rho)} | \Gamma_k^{(t,\rho)})] \\
&> 1 - \sum_{t \in T} \sum_{\rho \in R_t(\delta_t)} \frac{1}{|\mathscr{F}| - 1} \\
&= 1 - \frac{\sum_{t \in T} |R_t(\delta_t)|}{|\mathscr{F}| - 1} . \quad (5.4)
\end{aligned}
$$

Combining the inequalities (5.3) and (5.4), we have

$$1 - P_{ec} > \left(1 - \frac{\sum_{t \in T} |R_t(\delta_t)|}{|\mathscr{F}| - 1} \right)^{m+1} ,$$

that is,

$$P_{ec} < 1 - \left(1 - \frac{\sum_{t \in T} |R_t(\delta_t)|}{|\mathscr{F}| - 1}\right)^{m+1}.$$

The proof is completed.   □

Applying Lemma 4.3 to Theorem 5.1, we derive the following corollary.

Corollary 5.1. *The failure probability $P_{ec}(t)$ of random linear network error correction MDS coding for each $t \in T$ satisfies:*

$$P_{ec}(t) < 1 - \left(1 - \frac{\binom{|E_t|}{\delta_t}}{|\mathscr{F}| - 1}\right)^{|J|+1} \leq 1 - \left(1 - \frac{\binom{|E|}{\delta_t}}{|\mathscr{F}| - 1}\right)^{|J|+1}.$$

The failure probability P_{ec} of random linear network error correction MDS coding for the network G satisfies:

$$P_{ec} < 1 - \left(1 - \frac{\sum_{t \in T} \binom{|E_t|}{\delta_t}}{|\mathscr{F}| - 1}\right)^{|J|+1} \leq 1 - \left(1 - \frac{\sum_{t \in T} \binom{|E|}{\delta_t}}{|\mathscr{F}| - 1}\right)^{|J|+1}.$$

However, in practice, we sometimes need general linear network error correction codes instead of the network MDS codes. That is, we only need the codes satisfying that its minimum distance $d_{min}^{(t)} \geq \beta_t + 1$ for some nonnegative integer β_t with $\beta_t \leq \delta_t$. It is partly because usually the field size required by general linear network error correction codes is smaller than that of network MDS codes. Hence, we should also discuss the random method for constructing general linear network error correction codes. Similarly, we define the failure probabilities for random linear network error correction codes as follows.

Definition 5.2. Let G be a single source multicast network, $\mathbf{C}$ be a random linear network error correction code on G, and $d_{min}^{(t)}$ be the minimum distance at sink node t. Define that

- $P_{ec}(t, \beta_t) \triangleq Pr(\{\dim(\Phi(t)) < \omega\} \cup \{d_{min}^{(t)} < \beta_t + 1\})$, that is the probability that the code $\mathbf{C}$ cannot either be decoded or satisfy that the error correction capacity $d_{min}^{(t)} \geq \beta_t + 1$ at the sink node t;
- $P_{ec}(\beta_t) \triangleq Pr(\{ \mathbf{C} \text{ is not regular }\} \cup \{\exists t \in T \text{ such that } d_{min}^{(t)} < \beta_t + 1\})$, that is the probability that the regular linear network error correction codes with $d_{min}^{(t)} \geq \beta_t + 1$ cannot be constructed by the random method.

For the above two probabilities, we have the following results.

Theorem 5.2. *Let G be a single source multicast network, the minimum cut capacity for sink node $t \in T$ be C_t and the information rate be ω symbols per unit time satisfying $\omega \leq \min_{t \in T} C_t$. Using random method to construct a linear network error correction code, then*

- *for each $t \in T$ and $\beta_t \leq \delta_t$,*

$$P_{ec}(t, \beta_t) \leq \frac{|R_t(\beta_t)|\binom{\delta_t - \beta_t + |J| + 1}{|J|}}{(|\mathscr{F}| - 1)^{\delta_t - \beta_t + 1}};$$

- *for the network G,*

$$P_{ec}(\beta_t) \leq \sum_{t \in T} \frac{|R_t(\beta_t)|\binom{\delta_t - \beta_t + |J| + 1}{|J|}}{(|\mathscr{F}| - 1)^{\delta_t - \beta_t + 1}}.$$

Remark 5.1. Both Theorems 5.1 and 5.2 above imply that these failure probabilities can become arbitrarily small when the size of the base field $\mathscr{F}$ is sufficiently large.

For random linear network error correction codes, we know that the minimum distance of the code at each sink node are functions of the random local encoding kernels. Therefore, we use $D_{\min}^{(t)}$ to denote the minimum distance of random linear network error correction codes at a sink node $t \in T$ where the capital letter indicates that it is a random variable while the lower case letter is used for deterministic codes. Obviously, the Singleton bound tells us that $D_{\min}^{(t)}$ takes values in $\{1, 2, \cdots, \delta_t + 1\}$. For a code with the minimum distance $d_{\min}^{(t)}$ at the sink node t, $\delta_t + 1 - d_{\min}^{(t)}$ is called the *degradation* of the code at t. We are interested in the probability mass function of $D_{\min}^{(t)}$. Then the following conclusions are presented.

Corollary 5.2. *For a single source multicast network $G = (V, E)$, let the minimum cut capacity for the sink node $t \in T$ be C_t, the information rate be ω symbols per unit time satisfying $\omega \leq \min_{t \in T} C_t$, and $\delta_t = C_t - \omega$ be the redundancy of the code for a sink $t \in T$. For a given positive integer $d \geq 0$, the random linear network error correction codes satisfy:*

$$Pr(D_{\min}^{(t)} < \delta_t + 1 - d) \leq \frac{|R_t(\delta_t - d)|\binom{d + |J| + 1}{|J|}}{(|\mathscr{F}| - 1)^{d+1}},$$

and

$$Pr(D_{\min}^{(t)} \geq \delta_t + 1 - d, \forall t \in T) \geq 1 - \sum_{t \in T} \frac{|R_t(\delta_t - d)|\binom{d + |J| + 1}{|J|}}{(|\mathscr{F}| - 1)^{d+1}}.$$

This corollary leads to an upper bound on the field size required for the existence of linear network error correction codes with degradation at most d. On the other hand, Theorem 4.5 have shown a lower bound on the field size, i.e., $|\mathscr{F}| \geq \sum_{t \in T} |R(\beta_t)|$. Therefore, we derive the following result by combining them.

Corollary 5.3. *If the size of the base field $\mathscr{F}$ satisfies the following condition:*

$$|\mathscr{F}| \geq \min\left\{\sum_{t \in T} |R_t(\delta_t - d)|, \ 2 + \left[\sum_{t \in T} |R(\delta_t - d)|\binom{d + |J| + 1}{|J|}\right]^{\frac{1}{d+1}}\right\},$$

then there exists a regular linear network error correction code having degradation at most d at all sink nodes $t \in T$.

When $d = 0$, it is readily seen that

$$\sum_{t \in T} |R_t(\delta_t - d)| = \sum_{t \in T} |R_t(\delta_t)|$$

$$< 2 + (|J| + 1) \sum_{t \in T} |R_t(\delta_t)|$$

$$= 2 + \left[\sum_{t \in T} |R_t(\delta_t - d)| \binom{d + |J| + 1}{|J|} \right]^{\frac{1}{d+1}}.$$

This means that, for network MDS codes, Corollary 5.3 cannot give a smaller field size. But, for $d \geq 1$, the size bounds $2 + \left[\sum_{t \in T} |R_t(\delta_t - d)| \binom{d+|J|+1}{|J|} \right]^{\frac{1}{d+1}}$ and $\sum_{t \in T} |R_t(\delta_t - d)|$ have no deterministic relations. We will illustrate this point through the following example.

Example 5.1. For network G_2 shown by Fig. 5.1 below, let $\omega = 2$, and then $\delta_t = C_t - \omega = 2$.

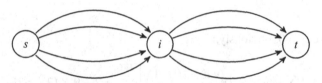

Fig. 5.1 Network G_2 with $|T| = 1, |J| = 1, C_t = 4$

- In the case $d = 0$, it is clear that

$$2 + \left[\sum_{t \in T} |R_t(\delta_t - d)| \binom{d + |J| + 1}{|J|} \right]^{\frac{1}{d+1}} = 2 + 2|R_t(2)| > |R_t(2)|.$$

- In the case $d = 1$, a simple calculation gives

$$\sum_{t \in T} |R_t(\delta_t - d)| = |R_t(1)| = 8,$$

and

$$2 + \left[\sum_{t \in T} |R_t(\delta_t - d)| \binom{d + |J| + 1}{|J|} \right]^{\frac{1}{d+1}} = 2 + \sqrt{24} < 2 + 5 = 7.$$

This shows that in this case

$$2 + \left[\sum_{t \in T} |R_t(\delta_t - d)| \binom{d + |J| + 1}{|J|} \right]^{\frac{1}{d+1}} < \sum_{t \in T} |R_t(\delta_t - d)|.$$

Nevertheless, for the network G_3 shown by Fig. 5.2, let $\omega = 2$, which shows $\delta_t = C_t - \omega = 2$.

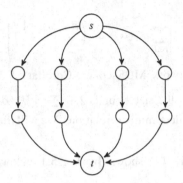

Fig. 5.2 Network G_3 with $|T| = 1$, $|J| = 8$, $C_t = 4$

- In the case $d = 0$, obviously,

$$2 + \left[\sum_{t \in T} |R_t(\delta_t - d)| \binom{d + |J| + 1}{|J|} \right]^{\frac{1}{d+1}} = 2 + 9|R_t(2)| > |R_t(2)|.$$

- In the case $d = 1$, after a simple calculation, we deduce that

$$\sum_{t \in T} |R_t(\delta_t - d)| = |R_t(1)| = 12,$$

and

$$2 + \left[\sum_{t \in T} |R_t(\delta_t - d)| \binom{d + |J| + 1}{|J|} \right]^{\frac{1}{d+1}}$$
$$= 2 + \left[|R_t(1)| \binom{1 + 8 + 1}{8} \right]^{\frac{1}{2}}$$
$$= 2 + (12 \times 45)^{\frac{1}{2}} \geq 20.$$

Therefore,

$$2 + \left[\sum_{t \in T} |R_t(\delta_t - d)| \binom{d + |J| + 1}{|J|} \right]^{\frac{1}{d+1}} > \sum_{t \in T} |R_t(\delta_t - d)|.$$

Chapter 6
Subspace Codes

While random linear network coding is an effective technique for disseminating information in communication networks, it is highly susceptible to errors. The insertion of even a single corrupt packet has the potential, when linearly combined with legitimate packets, to affect all packets gathered by an information receiver. The problem of error control in random network coding is therefore of great interest.

For this noncoherent transmission model for random linear network coding, that is, neither the source node nor sink nodes were assumed to have knowledge of the channel transfer characteristic, Koetter and Kschischang [29, 30] formulated a totally different framework from previous approaches for network error control coding. They also focus on end-to-end error correction coding, where only the source and sink nodes apply error control techniques. Internal nodes are assumed to be unaware of the presence of an outer code and they simply create outgoing packets as random linear combinations of incoming packets in the usual manner of random linear network coding. In addition, we assume that the source and destination nodes have no knowledge of the topology of the network or of the particular network code used in the network. This is in contrast to the pioneering approaches for coherent transmission model, which have considered the design of a network code as part of the error control problem. The key observation of this new approach is that, under the unknown linear transformation applied by random network coding, the only property of the transmitted packets that is preserved is their row space. Thus, information is encoded in the choice of a subspace rather than a specific matrix. The receiver observes a subspace, given by the row space of the received packets, which may be different from the transmitted space when packet errors occur. A metric is proposed to account for the discrepancy between transmitted and received spaces, and after that a new coding theory based on this metric is developed [7–9, 11–13, 27, 30, 32, 36, 37, 40, 42, 46, 47] etc.

X. Guang and Z. Zhang, *Linear Network Error Correction Coding*, SpringerBriefs in Computer Science, DOI 10.1007/978-1-4939-0588-1_6, © The Author(s) 2014

6.1 Channel Models

Let $q \geq 2$ be a power of a prime. In this chapter, all vectors and matrices have components in the finite field $\mathbb{F}_q$. We further use $\mathbb{F}_q^{n \times m}$ to denote the set of all $n \times m$ matrices over $\mathbb{F}_q$ and we set $\mathbb{F}_q^n = \mathbb{F}_q^{n \times 1}$. Particularly, $v \in \mathbb{F}_q^n$ is an n-length column vector and $v \in \mathbb{F}_q^{1 \times m}$ is an m-length row vector.

We first review the basic model for single-source random linear network coding mentioned above and consider a point-to-point communication network with a single source node and a single sink node. Generalization to single-source multicast is straightforward. Each edge in the network is assumed to transport, free of errors, a packet of M symbols in the finite field $\mathbb{F}_q$. During each transmission generation, the source node formats the information to be transmitted into n packets $X_1, X_2, \cdots, X_n \in \mathbb{F}_q^{1 \times M}$, which are regarded as incoming packets for the source node. Whenever a node (including the source) has a transmission opportunity, it produces an outgoing packet as a random $\mathbb{F}_q$-linear combination of all the incoming packets it has until then received. The sink node gathers N packets $Y_1, Y_2, \cdots, Y_N \in \mathbb{F}_q^{1 \times M}$ and tries to recover the original packets $X_1, X_2, \cdots, X_n$, where each Y_j is formed as

$$Y_j = \sum_{i=1}^{n} a_{ji} X_i,$$

with unknown and randomly chosen coefficients $a_{ji} \in \mathbb{F}_q$. Moreover, let X denote an $n \times M$ matrix whose rows are the transmitted packets $X_1, X_2, \cdots, X_n$ and, similarly, let Y denote an $N \times M$ matrix whose rows are the received packets $Y_1, Y_2, \cdots, Y_N$. Since all packet operations are linear over $\mathbb{F}_q$, then, regardless of the network topology, the matrix X of transmitted packets and the matrix Y of received packets can be related as

$$Y = AX, \tag{6.1}$$

where $A = [a_{ij}]$ is an $N \times n$ matrix corresponding to the overall linear transformation applied by the network.

Before considering the errors, we remark that this model encompasses a variety of situations:

- The network may have cycles or delays. Since the overall system is linear, expression (6.1) will be true regardless of the network topology.
- The network could be wired or wireless. Broadcast transmissions in wireless networks may be modeled by constraining each internal node to send exactly the same packet on each of its outgoing edges.
- The source node may transmit more than one generation (a set of n packets). In this case, we assume that each packet carries a label identifying the generation to which it corresponds and those packets from different generations are processed separately throughout the network.

- The network topology may be time-varying as nodes join and leave, and connections are established and lost. In this case, we assume that each network edge is the instantiation of an actual successful packet transmission.
- The network may be used for multicast. There may be more than one sink node. Again, expression (6.1) applies; however, the matrix A may be different for distinct sink nodes as described above.

Now, let us extend this model to incorporate packet errors. Consider that packet errors may occur in any edge of the network. Suppose the edges in the network are indexed from 1 to l, and let $Z_i \in \mathbb{F}_q^{1 \times M}$ denote the error packet occurred on edge $i \in \{1, 2, \cdots, l\}$. The application of an error packet is modeled as follows. We assume that, for each edge i, the node transmitting on that edge first creates a prescribed packet $P_{\text{in},i} \in \mathbb{F}_q^{1 \times M}$ following the procedure described above. Then, an error packet $Z_i \in \mathbb{F}_q^{1 \times M}$ is added to $P_{\text{in},i}$ in order to produce the outgoing packet on this edge, i.e., $P_{\text{out},i} = P_{\text{in},i} + Z_i$. Note that any arbitrary outgoing packet $P_{\text{out},i}$ can be formed simply by choosing $Z_i = P_{\text{out},i} - P_{\text{in},i}$. In this case, each received packet Y_j is formed as

$$Y_j = \sum_{i=1}^{n} a_{ji} X_i + \sum_{i=1}^{l} b_{ji} Z_i,$$

similarly, with unknown and randomly chosen coefficients $a_{ji}, b_{ji} \in \mathbb{F}_q$.

Let Z be an $l \times M$ matrix whose rows are the error packets $Z_1, Z_2, \cdots, Z_l$. By linearity of the network, we can write

$$Y = AX + BZ, \tag{6.2}$$

where $B = [b_{ji}]$ is an $N \times l$ matrix corresponding to the overall linear transformation applied to $Z_1, Z_2, \cdots, Z_l$ on route to the destination. Note that $Z_i = 0$ means that no corrupt packet was injected at edge i. Thus, the number of nonzero rows of Z, denoted by $\text{wt}(Z)$, gives the total number of (potentially) corrupt packets injected in the network. Note that it is possible that a nonzero error packet happens to be in the row space of X, in which case it is not really a corrupt packet. Eq. (6.2) is the basic model of a channel induced by random linear network coding, and it is referred as the *random linear network coding channel* (RLNCC). The channel input and output alphabets are given by $\mathbb{F}_q^{n \times M}$ and $\mathbb{F}_q^{N \times M}$, respectively.

Let $\mathscr{P}(\mathbb{F}_q^M)$ denote the set of all subspaces of $\mathbb{F}_q^M$. For transmission via subspace selection, the source node selects a subspace $V \in \mathscr{P}(\mathbb{F}_q^M)$ and transmits this subspace over the RLNCC as some matrix $X \in \mathbb{F}_q^{n \times M}$ such that $V = \langle X \rangle$. The sink node receives $Y \in \mathbb{F}_q^{N \times M}$ and computers $U = \langle Y \rangle$, from which the sink node tries to infer to the transmitted subspace V.

In order to describe the transmission model from a subspace perspective, Koetter and Kschischang introduced "*operator channel*" as a concise model for random linear network coding. For integer $k > 0$, define a stochastic operator $\mathscr{H}_k$, called an "*erasure operator*", that operates on the subspaces of $\mathbb{F}_q^M$. If $\dim(V) > k$, then $\mathscr{H}_k(V)$ returns a randomly chosen k-dimensional subspace of V; otherwise, $\mathscr{H}_k(V)$ returns V.

Definition 6.1. An operator channel associated with the ambient space $\mathbb{F}_q^M$ is a channel with input and output alphabet $\mathscr{P}(\mathbb{F}_q^M)$. The channel input V and channel output U can always be related as

$$U = \mathscr{H}_k(V) \oplus E,$$

where $k = \dim(U \cap V)$ and E is an error space. In transforming V to U, we say that the operator channel commits $\rho = \dim(V) - k$ erasures and $t = \dim(E)$ errors.

6.2 Subspace Codes

In the following, we give some concepts of the theory of subspace codes.

Definition 6.2. Let $V, V' \in \mathscr{P}(\mathbb{F}_q^M)$. The subspace distance between V and V' is defined as

$$
\begin{aligned}
d_S(V,V') &\triangleq \dim(V+V') + \dim(V \cap V') \\
&= 2\dim(V+V') - \dim V - \dim V' \\
&= \dim V + \dim V' - 2\dim(V \cap V').
\end{aligned}
$$

It is not difficult to show that the above subspace distance is indeed a metric on $\mathscr{P}(\mathbb{F}_q^M)$. Furthermore, a subspace code is defined as a nonempty subset of $\mathscr{P}(\mathbb{F}_q^M)$. The minimum distance of a subspace code $\mathscr{C} \subseteq \mathscr{P}(\mathbb{F}_q^M)$ is defined as

$$d_s(\mathscr{C}) \triangleq \min_{\substack{V,V' \in \mathscr{C} \\ V \neq V'}} d_S(V,V').$$

Particularly, if the dimension of each codeword of $\mathscr{C}$ is the same, then $\mathscr{C}$ is said to be a constant-dimension code. Formally, let $\mathscr{P}(\mathbb{F}_q^M, n)$ denote the set of all n-dimensional subspaces of $\mathbb{F}_q^M$. A subspace code $\mathscr{C}$ is called a *constant-dimension code* if $\mathscr{C} \subseteq \mathscr{P}(\mathbb{F}_q^M, n)$. It follows that the minimum distance of a constant-dimension code is always an even number.

The minimum distance decoding problem for a subspace code $\mathscr{C}$ is to find a subspace $\hat{V} \in \mathscr{C}$ that is closest to a given subspace $U \in \mathscr{P}(\mathbb{F}_q^M)$, i.e.,

$$\hat{V} = \arg\min_{V \in \mathscr{C}} d_S(V,U). \tag{6.3}$$

A minimum distance decoder is guaranteed to return $\hat{V} = V$ if $d_S(V,U) < d_S(\mathscr{C})/2$.

If we wish to relate the performance guarantees of a subspace code with more concrete network parameters, we would like choose those parameters to be sufficiently general so that we do not need to take the whole network topology into account. So we make the following assumptions:

- The column-rank deficiency of the transfer matrix A is never greater than ρ, i.e., $\text{Rank}(A) \geq n - \rho$. It can be viewed as the number of erasures.
- The adversarial nodes together can inject at most t corrupting packets, i.e., $\text{wt}(Z) \leq t$, which can be regarded as the number of insertion of errors.

The following result characterizes the performance guarantees of a subspace code under our assumptions.

Theorem 6.1 ([42, Theorem 1]). *Suppose* $\text{Rank}(A) \geq n - \rho$ *and* $\text{wt}(Z) \leq t$. *Then, the above minimum distance decoding (6.3) is guaranteed to be successful provided* $2t + \rho < d_S(\mathscr{C})/2$.

6.3 Bounds on Constant-Dimension Codes

In context of network coding, constant-dimension codes are one simple but important class of subspace codes. Thus they are interesting and many bounds on them have been developed. We start this section by introducing some notation.

The q-ary Gaussian coefficient, the q-analogue of the binomial coefficient, is defined, for non-negative integers n and M with $n \leq M$, by

$$\begin{bmatrix} M \\ n \end{bmatrix}_q \triangleq \frac{(q^M - 1)(q^{M-1} - 1)\cdots(q^{M-n+1} - 1)}{(q^n - 1)(q^{n-1} - 1)\cdots(q - 1)} = \prod_{i=0}^{n-1} \frac{q^{M-i} - 1}{q^{n-i} - 1},$$

where the empty product obtained when $n = 0$ is interpreted as 1. Furthermore, it is well known that the Gaussian coefficient gives the number of distinct n-dimensional subspaces of an M-dimensional vector space over $\mathbb{F}_q$, i.e., $\begin{bmatrix} M \\ n \end{bmatrix}_q = |\mathscr{P}(\mathbb{F}_q^M, n)|$.

Definition 6.3. For an n-dimensional subspace $V \in \mathscr{P}(\mathbb{F}_q^M, n)$. The sphere $S(V, n, t)$ of radius t centered at V is defined as the set of all subspaces U that satisfy $d_S(U, V) \leq 2t$, i.e.,

$$S(V, n, t) = \{U \in \mathscr{P}(\mathbb{F}_q^M, n) : d_S(U, V) \leq 2t\}.$$

Lemma 6.1. *The number of spaces in $S(V, n, t)$ is independent of V and equals to*

$$|S(V, n, t)| = \sum_{i=0}^{t} q^{i^2} \begin{bmatrix} n \\ i \end{bmatrix}_q \begin{bmatrix} M - n \\ i \end{bmatrix}_q$$

for $t \leq n$.

Note that the size of a sphere $S(V, n, t)$ is independent of its center. For convenience, define $|S(n, t)| = |S(V, n, t)|$.

Let $A_q[M, 2d, n]$ denote the maximum number of codewords in a constant-dimension code with minimum subspace distance $2d$. The following are many bounds on $A_q[M, 2d, n]$.

Theorem 6.2 (Sphere-Packing and Sphere-Covering Bounds).

$$A_q[M,2d,n] \leq \frac{|\mathscr{P}(\mathbb{F}_q^M,n)|}{|S(n,t)|} \leq \frac{\begin{bmatrix} M \\ n \end{bmatrix}_q}{\sum_{i=0}^{t} q^{i^2} \begin{bmatrix} n \\ i \end{bmatrix}_q \begin{bmatrix} M-n \\ i \end{bmatrix}_q} < 4q^{(n-t)(M-n-t)},$$

where $t = \lfloor (d-1)/2 \rfloor$;

$$A_q[M,2d,n] \geq \frac{|\mathscr{P}(\mathbb{F}_q^M,n)|}{|S(n,d-1)|} > \frac{\begin{bmatrix} M \\ n \end{bmatrix}_q}{dq^{(d-1)^2} \begin{bmatrix} n \\ d-1 \end{bmatrix}_q \begin{bmatrix} M-n \\ d-1 \end{bmatrix}_q} > \frac{1}{16d} q^{(n-d+1)(M-d-n+1)}.$$

In [30], a puncturing operation in $\mathscr{P}(\mathbb{F}_q^M,n)$ is defined that reduces by one the dimension of the ambient space $\mathbb{F}_q^M$ and the dimension of each subspace in $\mathscr{P}(\mathbb{F}_q^M,n)$. According to using this puncturing operation repeatedly, the following Singleton-type bound is established.

Theorem 6.3 (Singleton-type Bound).

$$A_q[M,2d,n] \leq \begin{bmatrix} M-d+1 \\ \max\{n,M-n\} \end{bmatrix}_q.$$

Together with a useful bound on $\begin{bmatrix} M \\ n \end{bmatrix}_q$

$$\begin{bmatrix} M \\ n \end{bmatrix}_q < 4q^{n(M-n)},$$

it follows

$$A_q[M,2d,n] < 4q^{\max\{n,M-n\}(\min\{n,M-n\}-d+1)}.$$

Xia and Fu [46] (see also [9]) derived two Johnson type upper bounds by applying the classical Johnson bounds on binary constant weight codes. A binary constant weight code is a binary code such that every codeword has a fixed Hamming weight. Below it is shown that a corresponding binary constant weight code can be obtained from a given constant dimension code. Recall that $\mathbb{F}_q^M$ is the M-dimensional vector space over the finite field $\mathbb{F}_q$ and $\mathscr{P}(\mathbb{F}_q^M,n)$ denote the set of all n-dimensional subspaces of $\mathbb{F}_q^M$. Let $\mathbf{0}$ denote the all-zero vector in $\mathbb{F}_q^M$ and $\mathbb{F}_q^{M*} = \mathbb{F}_q^M \setminus \{\mathbf{0}\}$. Denote $N = q^M - 1$. Suppose all the vectors in $\mathbb{F}_q^{M*}$ are ordered from 1 to N.

Define the incidence vector of a subset $X \subseteq \mathbb{F}_q^M$ as

$$\mathbf{v}_X = [v_1 \; v_2 \; \cdots \; v_N] \in \mathbb{F}_2^N$$

where $v_i = 1$ if the ith vector of $\mathbb{F}_q^{M*}$ is contained in X, and otherwise, $v_i = 0$. For any two n-dimensional subspaces $X, Y \in \mathscr{P}(\mathbb{F}_q^M, n)$, it is easy to see that

$$w_H(\mathbf{v}_X) = w_H(\mathbf{v}_Y) = q^n - 1,$$

$$w_H(\mathbf{v}_X * \mathbf{v}_Y) = q^{\dim(X \cap Y)} - 1,$$

$$d_H(\mathbf{v}_X, \mathbf{v}_Y) = 2(q^n - q^{\dim(X \cap Y)}),$$

where

$$\mathbf{v}_X * \mathbf{v}_Y = [v_1 u_1 \; v_2 u_2 \; \cdots \; v_N u_N]$$

with $\mathbf{v}_X = [v_1 \; v_2 \; \cdots \; v_N]$ and $\mathbf{v}_Y = [u_1 \; u_2 \; \cdots \; u_N]$.

Let $\mathscr{C} \subseteq \mathscr{P}(\mathbb{F}_q^M, n)$ be an constant dimension code with minimum distance at least $2d$. From the above equations and the definition of constant dimension codes, the incidence vectors of the codewords in $\mathscr{C}$ form a binary constant weight code C, called the derived binary constant weight code of $\mathscr{C}$, which has the following parameters: length $N = q^M - 1$, size $|\mathscr{C}|$, minimum distance $2(q^n - q^{n-d})$, and weight $q^n - 1$. In other words, a corresponding binary constant weight code can be obtained from a given constant dimension code. Thus, using the classical Johnson bound I for this corresponding binary constant weight codes, the Johnson type bound I for constant dimension codes are obtained.

Theorem 6.4 (Johnson Type Bound I for Constant Dimension Codes). *If*

$$(q^n - 1)^2 > (q^M - 1)(q^{n-d} - 1),$$

then

$$A_q[M, 2d, n] \leq \left\lfloor \frac{(q^n - q^{n-d})(q^M - 1)}{(q^n - 1)^2 - (q^M - 1)(q^{n-d} - 1)} \right\rfloor.$$

Subsequently, similar to the Johnson bound II for binary constant weight codes, the Johnson type bound II for constant dimension codes are given.

Theorem 6.5.

$$A_q[M, 2d, n] \leq \left\lfloor \frac{(q^M - 1)}{(q^n - 1)} A_q[M - 1, 2d, n - 1] \right\rfloor.$$

Theorem 6.6 (Johnson Type Bound II for Constant Dimension Codes).

$$A_q[M, 2d, n] \leq \left\lfloor \frac{(q^M - 1)}{(q^n - 1)} \left\lfloor \frac{(q^{M-1} - 1)}{(q^{n-1} - 1)} \cdots \left\lfloor \frac{(q^{M-n+d} - 1)}{(q^d - 1)} \right\rfloor \cdots \right\rfloor \right\rfloor.$$

The Johnson type bound II slightly improves on the Wang-Xing-Safavi-Naini bound [45].

6.4 Code Constructions and Decoding Algorithms

In this section, we first describe several constructing approaches of subspace codes. In particular, some constructions allow us to obtain nearly-optimal subspace codes. And then, the decoding of subspace codes is introduced briefly.

6.4.1 Code Constructions

One type of the simplest construction of the asymptotically optimal subspace codes is to use rank-metric codes to be shown in the following. This construction was first proposed in [45], and then rediscovered to obtain a nearly-optimal Reed-Solomon-like codes in [30], which, actually, is a special case of the lifting construction [42] where the rank-metric code is a Gabidulin code [11]. And the construction was explained in [42] in the context of the subspace/injection distance.

A matrix code is defined as any nonempty subset of $\mathbb{F}_q^{n \times m}$. A matrix code is also commonly called an array code when it forms a linear space over $\mathbb{F}_q$.

Definition 6.4. For $X, Y \in \mathbb{F}_q^{n \times m}$, the *rank distance* between X and Y is defined as

$$d_R(X, Y) \triangleq \text{Rank}(Y - X).$$

Note that this rank distance is indeed a metric. In the context of the rank metric, a matrix code is called a rank-metric code. The minimum (rank) distance of a rank-metric code $\mathscr{C} \subseteq \mathbb{F}_q^{n \times m}$ is defined as

$$d_R(\mathscr{C}) \triangleq \min_{\substack{X, X' \in \mathscr{C} \\ X \neq X'}} d_R(X, X').$$

The Singleton bound for the rank-metric codes states that every rank-metric code $\mathscr{C} \subseteq \mathbb{F}_q^{n \times m}$ with minimum distance $d = d_R(\mathscr{C})$ must satisfy

$$|\mathscr{C}| \leq q^{\max\{n,m\}(\min\{n,m\}-d+1)}.$$

Codes that achieve this bound are called maximum-rank-distance (MRD) codes and MRD codes are known to exist for all parameters n and m and all $d \leq \min\{n,m\}$, irrespectively of the field size q.

Definition 6.5. Let $\mathscr{I} : \mathbb{F}_q^{n \times m} \mapsto \mathscr{P}(\mathbb{F}_q^{n+m})$, given by $X \mapsto \left\langle \begin{bmatrix} I_{n \times n} & X \end{bmatrix} \right\rangle$. The subspace $\mathscr{I}(X)$ is called the *lifting* of the matrix X. Similarly, if $\mathscr{C} \subseteq \mathbb{F}_q^{n \times m}$ is a rank-metric code, then the subspace code $\mathscr{I}(\mathscr{C})$, obtained by lifting each codeword of $\mathscr{C}$, is called the lifting of $\mathscr{C}$.

Definition 6.5 provides an injective mapping between rank-metric codes and subspace codes, and a subspace code constructed by lifting is always a constant-dimension code (with codeword dimension n).

Lemma 6.2. *Let* $\mathscr{C} \subseteq \mathbb{F}_q^{n \times m}$ *and* $X, X' \in \mathscr{C}$. *Then*

$$d_S(\mathscr{I}(X), \mathscr{I}(X')) = 2d_R(X, X'),$$
$$d_S(\mathscr{I}(\mathscr{C})) = 2d_R(\mathscr{C}).$$

This lemma shows that a subspace code constructed by lifting inherits the distance properties of its underlying rank-metric code. In particular, let $\mathscr{C} \subseteq \mathbb{F}_q^{n \times m}$ be an MRD code with $d_R(\mathscr{C}) = d$ and, without loss of generality, let $n \leq m$. Then $\mathscr{I}(\mathscr{C})$ is a constant-dimension code with dimension n, minimum subspace distance $2d$, and cardinality

$$|\mathscr{I}(\mathscr{C})| = q^{m(n-d+1)},$$

which gives a lower bound on $A_q[n+m, 2d, n]$. Comparing with the above Singleton bound, we see that the ratio of the upper and lower bounds is a constant depending only on q, thus demonstrating that this construction yields asymptotically optimal codes.

Besides the above lifting construction of subspace codes, there are some other approaches to construct subspace codes, particularly, constant-dimension codes. For instance, Etzion and Silberstein [7] provided a multilevel construction via rank-metric codes and Ferrers' diagrams; Kohnert and Kurtz [32] viewed the construction of constant-dimension codes as an optimization problem involving integer variables, and then obtained some codes by integer linear programming, and so on (refer to [7, 32] for details).

6.4.2 Decoding Algorithms

Similar to the decoding problem in classical coding theory, the decoding problem of the subspace codes is also how to efficiently find a codeword that is closest to a given subspace $V \in \mathscr{P}(\mathbb{F}_q^M)$ in subspace distance. Several algorithms have been proposed for implementing the decoding for different encoding approaches. In [30], Koetter and Kschischang first proposed an algorithm to decode lifted Gabidulin codes, that is said to be nearly-optimal Reed-Solomon-like codes in [30]. This algorithm is a version of Sudan's "list-of-1" decoding for Gabidulin codes. A faster algorithm was proposed in [42] which is a generalization of the standard decoding algorithm for Gabidulin codes. For other types of subspace codes according to different constructing approaches, some efficient decoding algorithms were also proposed such as [7, 47]. Further, some list-type decoding beyond the error-correcting capability also have been discussed, such as [36, 37]. Because of the limit of pages, we omit the details.

References

[1] R. Ahlswede, N. Cai, S.-Y. R. Li, and R. W. Yeung, "Network information flow," *IEEE Trans. Info. Theory*, IT-46: 1204–1216, 2000.

[2] H. Balli, X. Yan, and Z. Zhang, "On randomized linear network codes and their error correction capabilities," *IEEE Trans. Info. Theory*, IT-55: 3148–3160, 2009.

[3] N. Cai "Valuable messages and random outputs of channels in linear network coding," 2009 IEEE International Symposium on Information Theory, Seoul, Korea, Jun. 2009.

[4] N. Cai and R. W. Yeung, "Network coding and error correction," 2002 IEEE Information Theory Workshop, Bangalore, India, Oct. 20–25, 2002.

[5] N. Cai and R. W. Yeung, "Network error correction, part II: Lower bounds," *Comm. Info. and Syst.*, 6: 37–54, 2006.

[6] D. Charles, K. Jain, and K. Lauter, "Signatures for network coding," 40th Annu. Conf. Inf. Sci. Syst., Princeton, NJ, Mar. 2006.

[7] T. Etzion and N. Silberstein, "Error-correcting codes in projective spaces via rank-metric codes and Ferrers diagrams," *IEEE Trans. Info. Theory*, IT-55: 2909–2919, 2009.

[8] T. Etzion and N. Silberstein, "Codes and Designs Related to Lifted MRD Codes," *IEEE Trans. Info. Theory*, IT-59: 1004–1017, 2013.

[9] T. Etzion and A. Vardy, "Error-Correcting Codes in Projective Space," *IEEE Trans. Info. Theory*, IT-57: 1165–1173, 2011.

[10] C. Fragouli and E. Soljanin, "Network coding fundamentals," *Foundations and Trends in Networking*, vol. 2, no.1, pp. 1–133, 2007.

[11] E. M. Gabidulin, "Theory of codes with maximum rank distance," *Probl. Inform. Transm.*, vol. 21, no. 1, pp. 1–12, Jan. 1985.

[12] M. Gadouleau and Z. Yan, "Packing and Covering Properties of Subspace Codes for Error Control in Random Linear Network Coding," *IEEE Trans. Info. Theory*, IT-56: 2097–2108, 2010.

[13] M. Gadouleau and Z. Yan, "Constant-Rank Codes and Their Connection to Constant-Dimension Codes," *IEEE Trans. Info. Theory*, IT-56: 3207–3216, 2012.

[14] C. Gkantsidis and P. Rodriguez, "Cooperative security for network coding file distribution," IEEE INFOCOM 2006, Barcelona, Spain, April 23–29, 2006.

[15] X. Guang and F.-W. Fu, "The Average Failure Probabilities of Random Linear Network Coding", *IEICE Trans. Fundamentals, Communications and Computer Sciences*, Vol. E94-A, No. 10, pp. 1991–2001, Oct. 2011.

[16] X. Guang and F.-W. Fu, "On failure probabilities of random linear network coding," to be submitted.

[17] X. Guang, F.-W. Fu, and Z. Zhang, "Construction of Network Error Correction Codes in Packet Networks", NetCod 2011, Beijing, China, July 25–27, 2011.

[18] X. Guang, F.-W. Fu, and Z. Zhang, "Construction of Network Error Correction Codes in Packet Networks," *IEEE Trans. Info. Theory*, IT-59: 1030–1047, 2013.

[19] T. Ho, R. Koetter, M. Médard, M. Effros, J. Shi, and D. Karger, "A random linear network coding approach to multicast," *IEEE Trans. Info. Theory*, IT-52: 4413–4430, 2006.

[20] T. Ho and D. S. Lun, *Network Coding: An Introduction*. Cambridge, U.K.: Cambridge Univ. Press, 2008.

[21] T. Ho, B. Leong, R. Koetter, M. Médard, M. Effros, and D. R. Karger, "Byzantine modification detection in multicast networks with random network coding," *IEEE Trans. Info. Theory*, IT-54: 2798–2803, 2008.

[22] T. Ho, M. Médard, J. Shi, M. Effros, and D. R. Karger, "On randomized network coding," 41st Annual Allerton Conference Communication, Control, and Computing, Monticello, IL, Oct. 2003.

[23] S. Jaggi, M. Langberg, T. Ho, and M. Effros, "Correction of adversarial errors in networks," 2005 IEEE International Symposium on Information Theory, Adelaide, Australia, 2005.

[24] S. Jaggi, M. Langberg, S. Katti, T. Ho, D. Katabi, and M. Médard, "Resilient network coding in the presence of Byzantine adversaries," IEEE INFOCOM 2007, Anchorage, AK, May 2007.

[25] S. Jaggi, P. Sanders, P. A. Chou, M. Effros, S. Egner, K. Jain, and L. M. G. M. Tolhuizen, "Polynomial time algorithms for multicast network code construction," *IEEE Trans. Info. Theory*, IT-51: 1973–1982, 2005.

[26] E. Kehdi and B. Li, "Null Keys: Limiting Malicious Attacks via Null Space Properties of Network Coding," IEEE INFOCOM 2009, Rio de Janeiro, Brazil, April 20–25, 2009.

[27] A. Khaleghi, D. Silva, and F. R. Kschischang, "Subspace codes," in *Cryptography and Coding 2009*, M. G. Parker Ed., Lecture Notes in Computer Science, vol. 5921, pp. 1–21, 2009.

[28] M. Kim, M. Médard, J. Barros, and R. Kotter, "An Algebraic Watchdog for Wireless Network Coding," 2009 IEEE International Symposium on Information Theory, Seoul, Korea, 2009.

[29] R. Koetter and F. R. Kschischang, "Coding for errors and erasures in random network coding," 2007 IEEE International Symposium on Information Theory, Nice, France, Jun. 2007.

[30] R. Koetter and F. Kschischang, "Coding for errors and erasures in random network coding," *IEEE Trans. Info. Theory*, IT-54: 3579–3591, 2008.

[31] R. Koetter and M. Médard, "An algebraic approach to network coding," *IEEE/ACM Trans. Networking*, 11: 782–795, 2003.

[32] A. Kohnert and S. Kurz, "Construction of large constant dimension codes with a prescribed minimum distance," *Mathematical Methods in Computer Science: Essays in Memory of Thomas Beth*, pp. 31–42, 2008.

[33] S.-Y. R. Li, R. W. Yeung, and N. Cai, "Linear network coding," *IEEE Trans. Info. Theory*, IT-49: 371–381, 2003.

[34] S. Lin and D. J. Costello. *Error Control Coding: fundamentals and applications*. Pearson Prentice Hall, 2nd edition, 2004.

[35] F. MacWilliams and N. Sloane. *The Theory of Error-Correcting Codes*. North-Holland publishing, 1978.

[36] H. Mahdavifar and A. Vardy, "Algebraic List-Decoding of Subspace Codes with Multiplicities," 49th Annual Allerton Conference Communication, Control, and Computing, Illinois, USA, Sep. 2011.

[37] H. Mahdavifar and A. Vardy, "List-decoding of Subspace Codes and Rank-Metric Codes up to Singleton Bound," 2012 IEEE International Symposium on Information Theory, Cambridge, USA, July 2012.

[38] R. Matsumoto, "Construction algorithm for network error-correcting codes attaining the singleton bound," *IEICE Trans. Fundamentals*, vol. E90-A, no. 9, pp. 1729–1735, Nov. 2007.

[39] M. J. Siavoshani, C. Fragouli, and S. Diggavi, "On locating byzantine attackers," NetCod 2008, Hong Kong, China, Jan. 2008.

[40] D. Silva, "Error Control for Network Coding," Ph.D. dissertation, University of Toronto, 2009.

[41] D. Silva and F. R. Kschischang, "Using rank-metric codes for error correction in random network coding," 2007 IEEE International Symposium on Information Theory, Nice, France, June 2007.

[42] D. Silva, F. R. Kschischang, and R. Kötter, "A Rank-Metric Approach to Error Control in Random Network Coding," *IEEE Trans. Info. Theory*, IT-54: 3951–3967, 2008.

[43] D. Silva, F. R. Kschischang, and R. Koetter, "A rank-metric approach to error control in random network coding," IEEE Information Theory Workshop on Information Theory for Wireless Networks, Bergen, Norway, July 2007.

[44] D. Wang, D. Silva, and F. R. Kschischang, "Robust Network Coding in the Presence of Untrusted Nodes," *IEEE Trans. Info. Theory*, IT-56: 4532–4538, 2010.

[45] H. Wang, C. Xing, R. Safavi-Naini, "Linear authentication codes: bounds and constructions," *IEEE Trans. Info. Theory*, IT-49: 866–872, 2003.

[46] S.-T. Xia and F.-W. Fu, "Johnson type bounds on constant dimension codes,", *Designs, Codes and Cryptography*, 50: 163–172, 2009.

[47] H. Xie, J. Lin, Z. Yan, and B. Suter, "Linearized Polynomial Interpolation and Its Applications," *IEEE Trans. Signal Processing*, 61: 206–217, 2013.

[48] X. Yan, H. Balli, and Z. Zhang, "Decode Network Error Correction Codes beyond Error Correction Capability," preprint.

[49] S. Yang, "Coherent network error correction," Ph.D. dissertation, The Chinese University of Hong Kong, 2008.

[50] S. Yang, R. W. Yeung, and C. K. Ngai, "Refined Coding Bounds and Code Constructions for Coherent Network Error Correction," *IEEE Trans. Info. Theory*, IT-57: 1409–1424, 2011.

[51] S. Yang, R. W. Yeung, and Z. Zhang, "Weight properties of network codes," *European Transactions on Telecommunications*, 19: 371–383, 2008.

[52] R. W. Yeung, *Information Theory and Network Coding*. New York: Springer, 2008.

[53] R. W. Yeung, "Multilevel diversity coding with distortion," *IEEE Trans. Info. Theory*, IT-41: 412–422, 1995.

[54] R. W. Yeung and N. Cai, "Network error correction, part I: Basic concepts and upper bounds," *Communications in Information and Systems*, 6: 19–36, 2006.

[55] R. W. Yeung, S.-Y. R. Li, N. Cai, and Z. Zhang, "Network coding theory," *Foundations and Trends in Communications and Information Theory*, vol. 2, nos.4 and 5, pp. 241–381, 2005.

[56] R. W. Yeung and Z. Zhang, "On symmetrical multilevel diversity coding," *IEEE Trans. Info. Theory*, IT-45: 609–621, 1999.

[57] R. W. Yeung and Z. Zhang, "Distributed source coding for satellite communications," *IEEE Trans. Info. Theory*, IT-45: 1111–1120, 1999.

[58] Z. Zhang, "Network error correction coding in packetized networks," 2006 IEEE Information Theory Workshop, Chengdu, China, 2006.

[59] Z. Zhang, "Linear network error correction codes in packet networks," *IEEE Trans. Info. Theory*, IT-54: 209–218, 2008.

[60] Z. Zhang, "Some recent progresses in network error correction coding theory," NetCod 2008, Hong Kong, China, Jan. 2008.

[61] Z. Zhang, "Theory and Applications of Network Error Correction Coding," *Proceedings of the IEEE*, 99: 406–420, March 2011.

[62] Z. Zhang, X. Yan, and H. Balli, "Some key problems in network error correction coding theory," 2007 IEEE Information Theory Workshop, Bergen, Norway, Jul. 2007.

[63] F. Zhao, T. Kalker, M. Médard, and K. J. Han, "Signatures for content distribution with network coding," 2007 IEEE International Symposium on Information Theory, Nice, France, June 24–29, 2007.